# RELATIONSHIP IN LEARNING

# RELATIONSHIP IN LEARNING

by

Marjorie L. Hourd

HEINEMANN
LONDON

Heinemann Educational Books Ltd
LONDON  EDINBURGH  MELBOURNE  SINGAPORE
JOHANNESBURG  IBADAN  NEW DELHI
KUALA LUMPUR  HONG KONG  TORONTO
AUCKLAND  NAIROBI

ISBN 0 435 80441 3

Published by
Heinemann Educational Books Ltd
48 Charles Street, London W1X 8AH
Printed in Great Britain at The Pitman Press, Bath

# Contents

# Acknowledgements

Without the encouragement of Peggy Volkov and Anthony Beal I doubt whether this book would have taken shape. I am also very grateful to my friends and former colleagues, Geoffrey Hoare and Dick Tahta for helping me, in so many ways, to refresh my thinking.

I owe a great debt to Dr Volkov and Julia Webb for their meticulous care in clarifying the text and in proof reading; a work carried out in the spirit of Montaigne 'by way of conference and not of regency'.

MARJORIE L. HOURD

The author and publishers wish to thank the following for permission to reprint copyright material: Evans Bros for Chapter Nine, which appeared in association with the University of London Institute of Education and Teacher's College, Columbia University, New York as the article 'Guidance in Training Teachers' in 1955 *Year Book of Education* (eds. J. A. Lauwerys and Robert King Hall); Simon and Schuster Inc for the poem 'The day snow blew down from the black valley' from *There are Two Lives*, ed. Richard Lewis, translated from the Japanese by Haruna Kimura.

To Peggy Volkov

# Preface

The essays in this book which are arranged in three parts were written within the last twenty years for several occasions and have been gathered together under one title. In one way or another they have to do with relationship as this emerges between teacher and child, tutor and student, authorities and teachers, writers and readers, the child and the universe and so on. That the school is a network of relationships is a fact long recognized by sociologists; however these articles were all written on the assumption that the social and the personal need to be brought together more closely in our understanding, as indeed do sociology and psychology; and in the belief that we are members of one another and yet remain singular, belonging to ourselves. For example informal class structures such as team teaching and group work have much to recommend them, yet they can all too easily be employed to mask the unique contribution that each child brings to his work in school. In the first half of this century psychologists began to define individual differences; in the second half they have turned their attention as well to the person in himself. The accent in education is still quite clearly and rightly upon the different ways in which a child tries to gain the recognition of his teachers, his peers and society in general, but there is also a growing awareness of his desire to establish himself apart and in his own eyes. The trouble is that we are all inclined to take human nature for granted either as unalterable or as completely malleable without realizing that we are only in the process of becoming human and that there is much to learn about what a human being is, as something other than an aggregate of attributes and abilities which we persuade ourselves that we can measure. This means there is much to learn about what a teacher is other than an instructor and assessor; he must become a person in himself and grow in human qualities. The child's grasp of the material put before him depends very largely upon the quality and depth of the teacher's recreation of it in his own life and imagination.

It was in the belief that there is a poetry as well as a science of the classroom that in 1951 I wrote *Some Emotional Aspects of Learning*. When it was suggested that this small book should be republished along with a few related articles that had already appeared in several journals I was aware that some revision would be necessary in order to make the collection readable to myself as well as others. However in the event the essays remain substantially as they were originally, with only a few additions and omissions. Looking back over twenty years it would seem that ideas about the teacher-child relationship as an exchange deeply rooted in primary experience have not altered very much, but advances in the social, psychological and physical sciences have enabled us to interpret this experience in wider contexts. In fact it appears that thinking in general has undergone the kind of extension that makes it more than ever necessary to nourish its roots. So, taking the book as a whole, there are bound to be fluctuations of thought—including repetitions and contradictions some of which at closer view appear as ways of looking at similar ideas in shifting lights.

It was during the fifties in this country that the role of the teacher as personal guide to the child and adolescent was becoming more or less officially recognized through the setting up of schemes for counselling and guidance; yet we have only to compare the recommendations in the 1955 *Year Book of Education* which was entirely devoted to 'guidance'—a great step forward in its day—with the vast and highly specialized literature on the various aspects of counselling available today to realize that something like a revolution has occurred. All the same there are fears in some quarters lest the courses for counsellors opening up on all sides should underestimate the knowledge and intuition of teachers. One could of course reply that had these intuitions entirely succeeded in guiding children in their life and work as a whole then the counselling movement would not have been so necessary, though the complexities of school life at present do indeed demand more attention than most teachers have time to give them. Advisory services will be more and more required as time goes on and we must hope that these will examine the attitudes of the advisors as well as of the advised. Perhaps the existence of these services will highlight rather than obscure the proper and essential work of teachers which I try to describe in this book.

Of course the counselling movement in itself and by definition indicates a departure from authoritarian and rigid methods of control. There are signs that the work of inspectors and supervisors in general is being affected by changes in the psychological climate. These changes were already evident in 1955 in an account of an international conference for inspectors, organized by the New Education Fellowship. It soon became manifest in this conference that the difficulties which children and young people had in coming to terms with authority were also experienced to some extent by teachers and grown-ups. For example it was pointed out in the account written by the chairman of the conference, Professor Ben Morris, that contrary to the total intention members tried to insist upon a specified list of topics and an agreed agenda to work from. 'The permissive nature of the agenda,' he wrote 'was intended to reveal to participants our common human need which teachers and children share in a high degree . . . for both a recognizable structure, and the freedom of "the blank agenda", "the empty canvas", and also our common difficulties in making constructive use of freedom when it is offered to us.'[1]

In a lecture given at this conference as well as in an article contributed to the *Year Book* already mentioned, both

[1] *The New Era in Home and School,* June 1955, p. 170.

reproduced in Part II of this volume, I have tried to see inspectors and supervisors in the roles not only of assessors and advisers but also of artist observers, itinerant philosophers; people who serve the teacher's or student's sense of identity by bringing authority and freedom into the same context.

Since 1955 we have been driven by circumstance and the changing pattern of society as a whole to face many of the consequences of our failure to discover a good working relationship between authority and freedom which in other terms is a failure to appreciate the possibility of new alliances between dependence and independence. For instance by dwelling too exclusively upon the rebellious responses of youth we are apt to overlook a current paradoxical situation. At the same time as new forms of guidance are being attempted in the classroom a significant type of independence is developing among children arising from their access to sources of knowledge over which we grown-ups have little control. In many directions today children may have to voyage through strange seas of thought more or less alone, particularly where parents are concerned. Quite out of the blue one day a young boy drew me into a discussion on time. 'You know, don't you,' he remarked, 'that time on that clock is not true time. It is one we make up.' 'Perhaps,' I ventured in the pause he allowed to find out what kind of grown-up I was, 'perhaps we have to invent this clock in order to deal in ourselves with what you are calling true time. We have to find somewhere to plant ourselves.' 'That is just it,' he cried, and he went on excitedly to describe the space-time continuum as he was able to understand it. I did not get the impression that he was showing off but rather that he was trying to share with me, a visitor to the house, his cosmic sense of a new world in which he was privileged to be young, but a world too in which he did not want to feel lonely, for I sensed an awkwardness, the awkwardness we all feel with people upon whom we know ourselves to be dependent just as surely as we know that we are leaving them behind. Grown-ups not mature enough in themselves to understand the changing situation of children today may perversely join up either with immature over-protesting youth or with equally immature reactionary adults. The latter are likely to put the blame for disruption of any kind upon those flexible modes of education which alone can resolve these conflicts.

This flexibility is to be thought of as a quality of knowledge itself. We have to find a scale of thinking in the classroom that will allow for Freud and Einstein, and all that has been opened up through their pathfinding. Children may go beyond their teachers and their parents in many areas of investigation but they will look to them to preserve continuity. That ideas about relationship require a wider and deeper context than ever before is the assumption made in Part III of this book. With it goes the hope that renewed thinking will bring the curriculum closer to children's learning needs as expressed in contemporary life and culture. We must provide opportunities for science and art to merge within the pupils' own imaginations. To quote the French physicist, Jean Caron, 'Science has often evolved by producing a harmony between what is known to be true and what is felt to be true; and it is art that has usually provided the clearest testimony to the latter.'[1] Literature in particular among the arts enables us, as I hope this book testifies, to identify with the extraordinary persistence and force of man's struggle to understand and be understood; yet doubtless a similar claim can be made for most disciplines by those who are deeply interested in them. After all, it is learning that makes it possible to learn.

Exeter 1971                                                        M.L.H.

---

[1] *Man in Search of Himself*, translated by T. E. Anderson, George Allen & Unwin Ltd, 1967, p. 138.

Hear, Read, Mark, Learn and Inwardly digest.

*Collect. Advent II*

The field of human learning covers phenomena which range all the way, from the simple almost reflex learning of a child to avoid a hot radiator, to the complex process of insight by which a scientist constructs a theory.

*John Dollard and Neal E. Miller*

Man cannot persist long in a conscious state, he must throw himself back into the unconscious, for his root lies there.

*Goethe*

We are still the children of Descartes, and it is only here and there you will find a spirit who dares to replace that inexorable first proposition (cogito, ergo sum) with the words I am, therefore I can love.

*Lawrence Durrell writing of the poet,*
*philosopher, doctor, Georg Groddeck*

Nothing that is said, written or printed can ever mean anything in itself: for it is only a person who utters something—or who listens to it or reads it—who can mean something *by* it.

The ideal of a Knowledge embodied in strictly impersonal statements now appears self-contradictory, meaningless, a fit subject for ridicule. We must learn to accept as one ideal a knowledge that is manifestly personal.

Personal knowledge is fully determined, providing that it is pursued with unwavering universal intent.

*Michael Polanyi on 'Personal Knowledge'*

# Foreword

The following essays are about learning as it affects people in
their feelings. It is, of course, an endless topic. Then why have I
chosen to dwell upon the particular emotional aspects of learning
represented here? I have to confess that I do not know any
more than a poet knows why he wrote upon certain subjects at
certain times, except that his experience caused him to think and
feel like that. But, someone might object, an essay on education
is not the same thing as a poem. In a sense it is. Each is the
result of one person's thought and, therefore, the expression of one person's feelings, because every general idea that the
mind entertains contains also a core of individual significance,
and in the same way every personal experience holds as part of
its meaning what is true for all people. So that in order to bring
living and learning together we need constantly to have the
individual-near and the universal-remote in ideas in a state of
interchange. The teacher needs to do this as well as the poet,
but with a greater degree of consciousness. He has to be both an
artist and a psychologist, to allow a rich unconscious life to flow
within him and at the same time to be aware enough of its
direction to harness its power to the work he has to do.

It is wise too to be conscious of the fact that when we are
writing about children we are also writing about ourselves.
This is another aspect of the interchange between nearness and
remoteness. Less damage would have been done by educational
philosophers if they had realized more clearly how personal
their theories were. Plato might not have banished the poet and
Madame Montessori the fairy tale had they known how far

their conclusions were derived from their own hopes and fears. Yet if the educationist is to express himself freely, he is bound to produce prejudice along with principle. This is the poet in him. Then it is that he needs the help of psychology to enable him to understand himself far enough to be of real service to his pupils.

Does this seem to ask too much of the teacher? A great deal has always been demanded of him. Now more than ever. He is expected to be a human creative person and yet also to have this scientific knowledge of the sources of his humanity. But perhaps the task is not as formidable as it sounds; perhaps he became a teacher because this is what he always wanted to do, because he was a person who both wanted to get to know himself and also to get to know children.

Certainly it is not possible to say anything important about children unless one is prepared to know oneself in relation to them. For some time we have recognized the importance of the teacher-child relationship as a factor in learning, but we are only just beginning to understand that if the teacher is to put himself in the right position with children he must be in contact with the child in himself. This is something rather different from being 'child-like' or being 'interested in' children. Sometimes, in fact, child-study can be a way of avoiding the claims of the child inside, by focusing attention on the one in the classroom. But knowing what it is to be a child, by coming to terms with the child in ourselves, is knowledge of another kind because it involves recognizing the aggressive roots of personality, as well as the more benign sources of influence. As a result of this awareness, radical changes are bound to take place in our attitudes. All this requires a great deal of courage. But most teachers are very courageous and they are not likely to shirk their responsibilities once they know what they are. It is to these teachers that this book is addressed.

# CHAPTER ONE

# Learning Health and Learning Illness[1]

Pedagogists at one time taught us that learning was a method of impression, consolidation and expression. It would seem in this way as though the health of the mind were attained through a kind of digestive process of taking in, assimilating and giving out. There is a good deal in this way of looking at it, though it does not, of course, tell the whole story of how we learn. Nor perhaps were these educationists fully aware of the extent to which emotional factors were involved.

First there is the process of taking in. How intricate this is in the classroom. So much depends on the teacher and the way he gives out; on how he presents materials to work with, ideas to fasten upon, facts to absorb. This will be determined by his attitude to learning as a whole. He should be a presumptuous kind of person like Bacon who took all knowledge for his province; for it is from such arrogance that the humility of the generous giver develops. This does not mean that he must presume to know everything, as some teachers imagine, but he must be able to feel within himself a capacity for knowing most things, which is quite different. Most of us have not seen the Pope, nor do I myself know much about him, but I feel that I could see him if I wanted to and find out all about him in so far as his presence and these facts were available. We do our best teaching, not from limited supplies of knowledge but from the potential of all knowledge.

[1] The substance of this chapter also appeared in *The Bulletin of Education* (Association of Teachers in Colleges and Departments of Education), May, 1950, under the title of 'Knowing about Knowing'.

Let knowledge be to a teacher a kind of birthright in an aristocratic sense. Then let him select from it what he requires and hand over what is needed in a democratic sense. Thus learning asserts its aristocratic rights before it becomes a democracy. The teacher's first concern is with that province of learning which has given him personally most profound satisfaction, and this will have produced a feeling for the provinces which his mind reaches towards, but which may only become his in awareness as they become the possession of those whom he teaches and with whom he comes into contact. It is thus that arrogance changes to humility because it is through our own wisdom that others are made wise. How well teachers know this who watch their pupils outstrip them, but have the satisfaction of recognizing seeds that they sowed.

The teacher who teaches from the capacity for all knowledge and the one who uses bits and pieces of knowledge will influence children's learning differently. If we deal in limited supplies, either we are likely to feel afraid lest we run out, in which case we may become rigid and dictatorial, or else, for fear of exposing our ignorance, we may attribute to what we know special powers, and become precious and hold our methods inviolable. But the teacher who is in possession not only of what he knows but of what he does not know, will be able to treat knowledge not as something either exhaustible or inexhaustible, but as always replenishable. He will be able to reserve facts and also to be generous when necessary without fear of loss. From him children will gain the ability to wait for knowledge and to luxuriate in it as well. They will ask sensible questions because they know they will get adequate answers. In this way a kind of learning health is established.

Once ideas have been taken into the mind, the teacher's responsibility to some extent alters. They are now the child's possession in a way in which they could never belong either to the writer from whom they were taken, or to the teacher who from his own store has handed them over. The democratic act of sharing has established a new aristocracy; and so it goes on.

If we attempt to interrupt this rhythm, then we are disturbing the give and take between individual minds which is the most valuable source of life and learning. But what happens in the child's mind whilst this process of assimilation is taking place is not easy to determine, because it will be different for every one. Here the teacher needs to be content to wait and to watch to some extent, and to attend to his own resources. 'Always reading, never to be read,' said Alexander Pope, 'Always teaching, never to be taught,' would be just as true. The more we are assured of our own learning health, the more we can allow the child to develop at his own pace without constant anxiety and interference. It is the teacher who is anxious about his own giving who cannot trust the gift to be satisfactorily accepted. He has to keep asking questions and testing children to find out how much has gone in, in order to reassure himself. This is disastrous for the growing faculties of children. If we can wait for consolidation the child too can be more patient. He needs time and space in which to become aware of himself as a person, for he knows that within himself a kind of reconstruction of the universe is taking place. He feels more and more confident in relation to the macrocosm outside, as his own microcosm shapes and re-shapes itself to his needs. This gives him a sense of immense potentiality from which perhaps springs that feeling for all knowledge.

But I do not want to suggest that the teacher has no reponsibilities whilst these reconstructions are going on. Of course changes cannot take place in the mind without many corrections having to be made—errors and wrong judgements rectified, and often cherished fantasies rejected, and parental standards put to the test. None of this is easy; and here the teacher needs to know how to treat discards lovingly, and to accept ignorance as a part of knowledge. For we cannot expect children to relinquish their strongholds without some resistance. They share the reluctance of all true thinkers to give up old beliefs before the new ones are part of themselves. But in all this they will be greatly helped if the teacher is a person who can recognize confusion as a stage in clarification. We must respect chaos if we are to understand meaning.

In all children reactions against learning are to be expected at times. A child may become difficult on his own, or he may look round for some one to be led astray by, or to lead astray. It is often very difficult for a teacher to know what to do in these cases, because so often he sees in the child or the group the reflections of his own resistances. It is a good thing therefore if he looks at himself first and asks: 'Did I go too fast? Did I keep them waiting too long? Was I not sure enough of my material? Did I only know it in a dead kind of way? Was I unable to accept their mistakes?' But even if a class gets quite out of order owing to such miscalculations we must not consider that our control is lost or even weakened. Because, as well as these faults in ourselves, it is likely that the child was exploiting them for his own purposes. He needed the opportunity to resist us. If we can understand this in time and regain the confidence thus temporarily lost, we are likely to grip the class with a new control coming this time from a mutual breaking down of resistance.

But all rebellion is not of this healthy kind, and most teachers have to deal in their classes with a certain number of children whose learning digestions are so impaired that these re-adjustments are not possible. Such children we can say are learning-ill. They have not a strong enough framework within which to know and to find out. It is not a case of not knowing yet and being prepared to wait, nor even of putting off knowing until they gain more confidence. They refuse to know at all. Such children may become excessively difficult to control, very aggressive, unbearably noisy and cheeky, making constant messes of their own work or other people's, and so on. Sometimes there is an epidemic of this kind of behaviour and we can feel so discouraged that we want to give up teaching altogether.

It is obvious that some of these children will find adequate expression of themselves difficult. Others will have a great need of it, and it will help the ailing child to get on his feet again and regain confidence. All expression is a gesture to the world outside—asking permission to take it into ourselves and also to become part of it. When our expression is accepted within the expression of someone else, then our value to ourselves is greatly increased. In a lesson both teachers and children should share each other's satisfactions—for every child is to some degree a teacher, and every teacher learns from the experience of a lesson.

So we see that old slogan 'No impression without expression' had some truth in it, but many teachers made the mistake of thinking that this was a progress which they had to engineer. Half the lesson was taken with giving out and the other half with taking back, so that work resulted which had little to do with mutual experience. We all know those lessons where a story was told, or a poem read, and the class was directed immediately to draw or paint their idea of what it meant without any effort on the teacher's part to give a choice of time or material, or to participate in the work through suggestion, interpretation or encouragement. All work which is genuinely individual also bears marks of the teacher's personality. A child writes a poem which is his own, but it is not quite the same as the one which he would have written for another teacher. Everything we are given in class which is the child's real possession, will be in the nature of a special offering. The more we fail to see this, the more will the originality fall off, and the children will give what they think is expected.

I have tried to suggest in this essay that the process of learning in some of its aspects moves through impression and assimilation to expression, but that this can happen well or ill. At the same time I have suggested that health and illness are not entirely separate conditions.

Absence of illness is not a good definition of health nor does a well written essay without mistakes nor a well documented treatise neccessarily represent a cultural achievement. The inability to recognize the interrelation of health and illness causes us to seek for escapes and avoid the pain of illness, especially when we think society has become sick. This is what is happening too in education. We feel that we are in a dilemma and so a frantic search is going on for a way out. 'What has gone wrong here' we ask, 'and what has gone wrong there?' We want to pin down the responsibility. Would it not be wiser to realize the inevitability of conflict, and instead of seeking the precisions of this and that new system allow ourselves some of the privileges of doubt and uncertainty! For knowledge will only come to us whole if we are prepared to submit to the chaos and travail of knowing.

\*    \*    \*    \*    \*

We tend to think of health in terms of the state of ego-defences. We say it is more healthy when these defences are not rigid etc. . . . . But when we have reached this point we have not yet started to describe what life is like apart from illness or absence from illness. That is to say we have yet to tackle the question of what life is about.

D. W. Winnicott

## CHAPTER TWO

# Devotion and Doubt[1]

No teacher can escape the responsibility of being one, which means that he must have the courage to face young suggestible minds with the power of his own suggestiveness. It is no doubt because this is such a daring thing to do that some teachers seek ways of escape. They become instructors and hide behind facts, or organizers and hide behind methods (this latter is the more fashionable form of escape at present). But the true teacher knows that there is no way out. He accepts the paradox that genuine individuality is gained through suggestion, independence through dependence. He is neither an instructor, therefore, nor a director, but he is both an actor and a producer.

Socrates was this kind of a teacher. We are so familiar with the socratic method of reasoning that we are inclined to overlook the very subtle way in which the arguments were presented. Socrates had a dramatic instinct, with a feeling for the unities. He knew just where to molest a man in the street, just when to nudge him at a feast, at what point anyone was ready to listen to him. Far too much learning takes place in classrooms and lecture rooms. An educational institution of whatever kind should have a courtyard, quadrangle, garden or common-room where both teachers and taught can be rightly and properly molested. But the influence of Socrates had also a psychological foundation. He produced in men two attitudes of mind, one of devotion, and one of doubt, and these are the pre-requisites of learning. The art of suggestion depends very largely upon a

[1] This essay first appeared in *The New Era in Home and School*, January, 1951, under the title, 'Suggestion in the Class-room'.

combination of this dramatic and psychological insight, and this is why poetic treatments of the subject so often bring us closer to the heart of the mystery than the descriptions of the scientific investigators.

It has struck me that *The Tempest* is perhaps the most eloquent comment on suggestion in our literature, as well as being many other things besides, for it is an allegorical play, containing many meanings and yielding to many interpretations. In one aspect of his personality, Prospero is the arch-teacher. The fact that he worked on a magic island in a special robe and conjured spirits shows just how well Shakespeare understood the job.

All schools should be enchanted islands both to teachers and taught, and whether the master dons a gown or not, the children will regard his clothes as belonging to him in a special way. I can remember the clothes of nearly all my mistresses, and in particular the very beautiful overalls of one of the Froebel staff. She had at least half a dozen of these magic robes, and I think I regarded her as a conjuror. I was very much afraid of her, but I have to re-member that throughout my life I have loved bright embroidery on grey linen, and this was the colour scheme of the pinafore I admired most. But I could not recognize the liking that was mixed up in my disliking, because she was not the kind of person to understand all this. She was a moralist, which was a great pity for she might have done much with that conjuring personality and those overalls.

It is the teacher like Socrates who can unite our doubt and our devotion from whom we can learn most. Prospero was a teacher like this, too, but he could not have achieved so much in his work of re-education were it not for Ariel. Ariel is the embodiment of the power of suggestion. In fact Socrates and Ariel were very much alike in the way they went about things. They worked with a mixture of ruthlessness and grace. Let us watch Ariel at his job.

After he had sunk the vessel in which the Neapolitan wedding party was sailing, he dispersed the company about the island, and then went round whispering things in their ears when they were in the right mood to take what he had to say. Ferdinand, it will be remembered, was in a particularly sorry state because he had just seen his father drowned or so he thought. There he sat, we are told, in an odd angle of the isle, cooling the air with sighs and his arms folded in a sad knot: a faithful picture of depression. Ariel chose this moment to draw him to contemplate his sorrow to some purpose. But he did not go up to him and shake him by the shoulders and say: 'Your father is at the bottom of the sea, so get up and do something'. That 'pull yourself together' attitude never does any good when you are in a deep state of anguish. He used suggestion. First he sang about the fairies dancing on the yellow sands. He put his pupil into an enchanted state of mind, but with a warning that he would have to wake up from it, just as all the spirits of the night are called in from play at cock-crow when watch-dogs bark and the daylight world takes over.

But what a difficult stage in our education this is, that stage when we do not quite know whether we sleep or wake, when sometimes the dream is so sweet that, like Caliban, we cry to dream again; at other times the dream has so disturbed us that we are only too glad to join the waking world. And that is the stage a child is in when he listens with rapt attention to a fairy story which has both entranced and disturbed him, and he asks: 'Is it true?' 'Did it really happen?' one of the most difficult questions we are ever asked to answer. Ariel knew how to use this moment, for whilst with the devotion of enchantment Ferdinand followed the music that crept by him upon the waters, Ariel decided to strike deeper, to reach the doubt that lay at the bottom of his mind, a doubt about his filial reactions to the thought of his father's death; for as soon as he takes the suggestion that his father is not only drowned but is also re-fashioned into the coral and pearl of the ocean-bed, then he is able to permit a sea-change to take place in the depths of his own mind, and to join the sea-nymphs in sounding the knell of that ugly doubt.

Full fathom five thy father lies
Of his bones are coral made

Those are pearls that were his eyes,
Nothing of him that doth fade
But doth suffer a sea-change
Into something rich and strange
Sea-nymphs hourly ring his knell.
                    Ding-dong.
Hark now I hear them. Ding-dong, bell.

Now he is ready for action. He sees Miranda, suffers the transfixion of love at first sight, but is very soon offering her the throne of Naples so recently vacated by his father. This behaviour, as we discover from the rest of the play, is entirely in keeping with his character. Ariel did not put any ideas into his head that were not there already. And this is just what happens in the mind of a child when he listens to stories and poetry, when he paints and draws; fantasy thus released does not render him powerless, but makes it much more possible for him to encounter the real world and its problems, and to do this in accordance with his own personality.

As we watch the power of suggestion in the world we discover what a complicated task it fulfils, which these occurrences in *The Tempest* so exquisitely condense. We see that is works from person to person through devotion and doubt, that it stirs the memory in unconscious sources, and that it results in expression and action.

Everybody is open to suggestion, but some people are more suggestible than others, and in different ways and at different times. We know for example that people who are ill are very suggestible, but so are people who are creative and imaginative, and also people who are in love—'the lunatic, the lover and the poet.' Suggestion is at its best educationally when neither our devotion nor our doubt is too strong, for we know how possible it is to love someone so devotedly that we do everything to prevent contrary feelings from gaining admittance, or we can put up such strong resistances that we will not give reason and understanding their rightful place. Every child in a classroom or student in a lecture room needs to feel that the teacher is speaking to him alone with special intent, but he must also be able to feel that he can refuse what is said to him if it does not seem to suit him. Inattention and the deaf ear are as appropriate in the classroom as rapt attention. And it is a good thing if the same person calls forth both attitudes. But it is unlikely that a child will feel safe in expressing his doubt or in breaking down resistances to learning if he cannot first express his devotion. The teacher with the fine overalls thought she had to improve and instruct me without realizing that first she had to relieve my fears and anxieties so that the sea-change could take place. We inhabited a magic island together to no purpose because she failed to accept the responsibilities of the magician.

Indeed, sometimes these responsibilities are very great, and especially when we are dealing with learning-illness, for it is at such times that suggestion may have a distintegrating effect. It is often the fear of this which prevents the teacher from using his personality to the full. And yet in all learning a certain amount of this disintegration must take place. Prospero knew this and so he caused Ariel to produce the tempest. His methods at times were certainly drastic. He boarded the king's ship and 'flamed amazement', so that they all felt 'a fever of the mad'; a few indeed 'played some tricks of desperation'. This was the thorough shaking up they got before they were submitted to the witchery of the island. Nor was this entirely pleasant, for Prospero played many tantalizing tricks upon them. He would spread forth a banquet and just when they thought they could eat their fill, he would find some quaint device to make it vanish. Or he would entertain them with insubstantial pageants and then melt them into air. All this before he chose that moment when he could 'bass their trespass' and work upon the guilt in their minds. 'Methought the billows spoke and told me of it', says Alonso after the feast has disappeared and he is so moved that he goes out with intent to drown himself, to do the thing which Ferdinand thought had already happened to him, which he thought had happened to Ferdinand.

> I'll seek him deeper than e'er plummet sounded,
> And with him lie there mudded.

But Prospero knew what effect his suggestion was having. He knew that the memory needs to be deeply stirred before

> Understanding
> Begins to swell, and the approaching tide
> Will shortly fill the reasonable shore
> That now lies foul and muddy.

It is, however, only with very sick people that such measures become necessary; but it may be that before any of us can remember and recollect our true selves a certain amount of distribution and dispersal has to take place, and some teasing and tantalizing as well. If doubt and contra-suggestibility gain the upper hand in a class this may be an important stage to be gone through, for so often such a period is followed by one of intense concentration and understanding, that is if the teacher has his Prospero robes on, and knows how to use his Ariel qualities to the best advantage.

Thus it was upon the memories of the Neapolitan lords that Ariel's suggestions worked so that they began to see the world around them in terms of their own moods and wishes. What seemed lush and lusty grass to the guileless Gonzalo was dried up and tawny to the guilty Antonio. And this was another necessary stage in their re-education. Not until they had so experienced things did their vision clear. Any suggestions which we make to children will most certainly have the same effect. We shall not put ideas into their heads, but make clearer and more conscious what is already there; but not before they have first worked through the shows and fantasies which are parts of their natures. This is why we can never go very far if we expect children to turn out what we think we have put in. Such an attitude breeds impatience too. 'I've said this once, I won't repeat myself.' 'How many times have I to tell you?' If you are a conjuror or an actor you will not mind how many repeat performances you give because no two audiences are ever the same, nor are any two contexts in the classroom, not even if you repeat yourself immediately, for suggestion works with Ariel-swiftness.

> Before you can say come, and go,
> And breathe twice.

And the second time you say the same thing, if you are careful to 'do your spiriting gently' and not show impatience, the mind takes the suggestion differently because more deeply. We should, however, realize that it is much more difficult for children to repeat themselves in class. Their answers are so often discoveries to themselves which they feel nervous of asserting, or what they say is a personal communication which if repeated seems to lose the joy of its immediacy. How frequently one has to bend over a child in class to catch the whispered answer. I think teachers may resent having to say things over and over again because they feel that their prestige is threatened. But the contrary is true. Only where order reigns can suggestion work through to freedom. Ariel had to obey 'the strong bidding' and 'high charges' of his task-master. Frequently he jibbed, was sulky or openly rebellious, but his sense of loyalty and service prevailed because his chief desire was to be free, and this he was promised when the educative task was over.

Here we meet again the paradox with which we began. The greater the dependence of the child upon the suggestiveness of the teacher whilst he is learning, the greater will be the independence which finally he gains; providing that the dependence admits doubt and resistance. Children cannot come into their own unless the Ariel quality of living is given its full rein. But this means that we must recognize, as Prospero did, the conflict in the minds of those we seek to educate, and more than this allow, too, for the conflict which is a quality of thought itself—a struggle between service and freedom which was part of Ariel's nature. For in every idea which comes into the mind, one part of it is seeking to return to the limbo of the elements where it had its beginning, and another part is seeking to gain consciousness and share in the work of culture and education. It is because of the existence of this conflict that we can never be liberated from the power of suggestion, but are subject to it, and will seek to subject it as long as we live. Prospero was not expressing a purely romantic idea, but a fundamental fact about the relation between unconsciousness and consciousness when he said:

> we are such stuff
> As dreams are made on; and our little life
> Is rounded with a sleep.

No doubt it has occurred to the reader that in emphasizing the personal level upon which suggestion works I have neglected the influence upon the child of materials and things, that also in thus laying stress upon the fantasy element in life, I have neglected the realities of the external world as a source of education. I have looked too long upon the dreams and have not given sufficient attention to the stuff upon which they are made, which not only consists of these unconscious wishes and needs, but also of the facts and happenings of our everyday lives. I once gave a class of children who were reading *The Tempest* the task of preparing a picture map of the island, depicting all the natural features of the place. As I watched the work grow and listened to their remarks I realized that whether we treated the 'still-vext Bermoothes' as one of the Bermuda islands or thought of them as only a dream-land washed by

> the foam
> Of perilous seas in faery lands forlorn

they nevertheless had the local habitation and the name which Shakespeare claimed for all products of the imagination: that if one landed on Prospero's island with text in hand one could find one's way about among 'the fresh springs, brine-pits, barren place and fertile' and not get lost, because one had a kind of compass. But these children soon began to see that although there was a wealth of detail to go into the map, yet all the time they were not able by this means to portray 'the subtleties of the isle'. These subtleties came from the effects of Prospero's art working on the imagination of the inhabitants. In the same way the materials that we put before children in the shape of paint and paper, pen and ink, wood and clay, specimens of all kinds and aids visual and auditory—all these will not yield their suggestions unless we not only select them but watch and help the child at work with them; and know how to answer when like Ariel he creeps up and says, 'Was't well done?' 'Have you corrected my essay?' We cannot leave him alone without a compass and this we regulate primarily from a knowledge of his natural instincts and understanding, too, of the 'sea-sorrow' he is bound to suffer. True we govern him also by our knowledge of the external world and its laws, but it was Caliban who showed Prospero where to find everything and Ariel who adapted it to his purposes. Try how we will we cannot escape the realities of psychic existence into the material world, which does not mean that this world is non-existent, nor that it has not purposes of its own. It is indeed one of the chief aims of education to discover what these are and to adapt to them.

I have been guilty in this article of belabouring *The Tempest* for the purposes of the argument and of neglecting the many other meanings in the text. A play can play many parts and so, of course, can a teacher. He is not likely to do really well in his magic robes if he wears them all the time. I have on occasions maliciously observed how reluctantly schoolmasters doff their gowns when they enter their own homes, where they know that authority and glamour are worn with a difference. Prospero took his off when he talked with Miranda.

Let us get rid of the myth that the schoolmaster is the same person in the classroom and outside. He is not. The danger lies in his inability to recognize his duality. There is always something a little unreal about the teachers who never leave their magic islands, and this is a problem for boarding schools to solve. But those who never feel any magic are in a worse position because they are not teachers at all, but either usurpers of the dukedom like Antonio or academic pedants like the one-time Prospero, whose books were 'dukedom large enough'. For every day to a teacher is like the time-span of a play. In the morning he sets out for the enchanted island, puts on his robes, opens up his bag of theatrical tricks, releases Ariel and begins. Then at the end of the day he folds up his staff, takes off his gown, abjures his rough magic and goes home to Milan.

\*     \*     \*     \*     \*

'I cannot refute your arguments, Socrates.' 'You cannot refute truth, my dear Agathon: to refute Socrates is nothing difficult.'
From *The Symposium of Plato*

We are not claiming to show how men think in Myths, but rather how the myths think themselves out in men and without men's knowledge.

Lévi-Strauss

# CHAPTER THREE

# Humour and Criticism[1]

When I was discussing the Prospero role of the teacher with a group of students, one of them remarked: 'But if one is conjuring one's own way in a classroom, and anyone comes in to observe the lesson then it goes flat immediately because it is not easy to joke it down as one always tries to do if the spell breaks.' What an important thing she had said. It does not appear that Prospero had a very highly developed sense of humour, nor were there any inspectors or supervisors on his island. But we know that a sense of humour and an ability to take criticism from outside are very valuable assets in a teacher, so it is obvious that the Prospero side of him does not tell the whole story.

How well teachers know that feeling when their omnipotent position is beginning to fail. In one part of themselves they are relieved because they know they are not really very powerful, but in another part they are fearful because authority must be maintained. If things have gone too far, something quite dreadful happens. The children laugh at them before they can get their joke in. They have to be very skilful if they are to rescue this situation by sharing the joke against themselves, because so often neither they nor the children have the least idea what it is about.

It seems as though in every classroom there exists a rather tricky situation between teacher and child. In general there is a tacit agreement between them that one is to expect obedience and the other is to obey. Yet in each child there lies a certain

[1] This essay arose from the concurrence of a student's remarks and my reading of Freud's paper on 'Humour' published in *Collected Papers*, Vol. V, No. xx (1950 edited by James Strachey—The Hogarth Press.)

cunning desire to seize the throne whenever an opportunity presents itself, to triumph if only for a brief time over this kingly being; whilst in each teacher lurks the fear that his underlings will usurp his power. Therefore in spite of the devotion and willingness to learn which a good teacher receives from his class, he knows all the time that these rebellious forces are present. So a tension develops which if properly regulated provides a most valuable stimulus to learning.

It is more than anything a sense of humour which achieves a balance of forces, so that incentives are not lost and yet energy is properly distributed. A teacher can exercise this humour in several ways:

1. He can make a joke about somebody outside the classroom or about something that occurs in the material of the lesson; or he can allow the children to do this.

2. He can laugh at himself and so give the class a chance to join in, and thus save himself the humiliation of the joke's arising without his permission.

3. He can laugh at the child or the class with the understanding that they can use the same weapon against him with impunity.

Now in all this a play is being acted which is a representation on an external stage of the drama which is going on inside us most of the time, the chief actors of which are parents and children. In the first case the teacher puts the class in the adult position along with himself, and the outsiders become the children over whom together they gain the ascendancy. In the second place he creates within himself a child at whom another part of himself laughs, and allows the children to identify themselves both with this child and the adult. It is as though he places himself as a child with the child upon the throne, and then steps back as an adult and watches, knowing that he can remove the little imposters at any moment, and he incites the child to usurp an adult role and watch the game as well. 'See', the teacher is saying, 'what a great joke this is, this rivalry between you and me. There is nothing terrifying in it at all.' If he uses the third method, it must include the possibility of the second or he is not playing the game, because he is assuming a superiority which he already has and at the same time takes from the child the right to rebel. This humiliation will cause the child to dam up energy in anger and revenge which should be free for the purposes of the lesson.

Let us see what happens when the joke fails altogether, and yet the parental authoritative role has also been abandoned. Something rather frightening occurs. The joke turns into a ghost. Sometimes this is so alarming to a class that they have no power to whip their rebellious feelings into laughter. They become silent and fall back as if they had indeed seen the spectre. The teacher has failed them on two counts. He is not the all-powerful parent who will protect their rebellious feelings, neither is he the good human parent who will turn their ogres into playthings. So the child is left alone with all his wicked intents. There is nothing to stop him from seizing the throne in reality not in sport. This is certainly no position for him to find himself in. We have indeed deserted him. It is not surprising that in the old miracle play the devil became a comic character, for we take every opportunity of reducing the pain of fear by gaining the pleasure of laughter.

Perhaps we can now understand why this healthy tension between jokes is upset if a person goes into the classroom in the position of Headmaster or Inspector. The teacher may become a child in his feelings and rebel against the position, especially when he is with his own class. (Incidentally nothing upsets parents more than to be made to feel small with their own children.) And this is where the head or inspector needs great understanding. Let him be sure when he goes to observe a lesson that he has the child within himself ready at hand so that his self-criticism and sense of humour can humanize the situation. Bacon wisely remarked that it was reserved for God and the angels to be lookers-on in this world. It is indeed a role we should only adopt with care and thought. The fear of inspectors is lessening in schools, partly because they are understanding their job better. The reason for this fear does not always lie with the inspector. There is a human tendency to put upon an outside authority deficiencies we find in ourselves. And what a vicious circle this can become. We can blame the head who does not leave us alone or the authority which denies us the right opportunities, or the ministry for making such and such regulations, or the government for appointing such a ministry. The larger the body the easier a scapegoat it makes. At last we may only be left with the power of evil in the world, and then we know that evil can exist nowhere but in man's heart, and so we are back where we began. There we must look for reformation. But even so we may seek to reform others rather than ourselves. All this does not mean that these people and authorities are innocent of using their power in the wrong way, but until we have examined our own motives in relation to them we are not in a position to estimate the extent of this influence.

There is undoubtedly still far too much patronage on the part of heads and inspectors. Authorities who treat their teachers as though they were children with orders and regulations mixed with condescending pats on the back are putting themselves in an illogical position. They are expecting teachers to exercise a role in the classroom which they are denying them in the school and educational system as a whole. Such bodies deserve what they get, resentful and dissatisfied workers. If less time were spent administratively supervising financial and material losses, and more were given to the wastage of the spirit, not only would the former take care of itself, but the profession would gain in status and dignity.

A teacher should be left by the head to govern his classes according to his own standards and to use his gifts to the best of his abilities. The function of the outside authority is to provide the materials and the room physically and mentally for this to happen. If the teacher fails, then he needs help and guidance and the exercise from the head or the inspector of the same sense of humour within the whole school situation as he himself is expected to use in the classroom. I sometimes think that this sense of humour is the most precious gift that a teacher can have, and people should certainly summon all they possess of it before they enter a school building, or any other section of the educational services.

*     *     *     *     *

If we turn to consider the situation in which one person adopts a humorous attitude towards others, one view which I have already tentatively suggested in my book on 'Wit' will seem very evident. It is this: that the one is adopting towards the other the attitude of an adult towards a child, recognizing and smiling at the triviality of the interests and sufferings which seem to the child so big.

We must recall the other, perhaps the original and more important situation in humour in which a man adopts a humorous attitude towards himself in order to ward off possible suffering.

Freud on *humour*

# CHAPTER FOUR

# Fact and Fantasy

A window cleaner came to the house where I was staying one day, and I noticed how the children of the neighbourhood followed him. They watched with bated breath and wide-open eyes as the ladder went up and the man with sure steps climbed to the top; and then slowly a few toddlers attempted the bottom rungs. One little boy was taken right up and looked in at his mother through the window to her intense delight and anxiety. I remarked on how he gathered the children of the neighbourhood round him and he smiled a Pied Piper smile and replied: 'I don't know what it is, but there's something about window cleaning for children; they follow me wherever I go.' He picked up his ladder and moved on to the next house, calling the children by name who trotted after him to see the mysterious rites once more performed. I knew that this window cleaner was a fortunate man because he was conscious that he had a job with something special about it. Also I felt that he was an educator. He was aware of a symbolic significance to his trade without being able to specify it. The world of fantasy and the world of reality were not separated but grew together in his understanding.

If only Plato had known what the window cleaner knew, but he did not. Somewhere in his mind he was muddled about fact and fantasy and he would have begun to argue about real ladders and symbolic ladders as he did about tables. He would only have been satisfied that watching the window cleaner was an *education* for children if they were instructed as early as possible in the manufacture and right use of ladders! Not that he was a materialist or a philistine: far from it. He admired the poets greatly, yet, because he esteemed what he called 'truth' more, he shut them out of his republic. There was no alternative for a true citizen. Either one must close one's ears to their siren voices or be lost to a lotus land.

'But why bring Plato into this argument?' it might be asked by the modern educator. 'With our knowledge of the unconscious, we are not likely to fall into the platonic trap. Our nursery and infant teachers are well aware of the meaning of fantasy for the child. We have introduced activity methods on a large scale and poetry and art are not banished from our Primary and Secondary schools. In fact, we are encouraged in these ways of teaching.' All this is true; but if educationally we had shed this Platonic fallacy I suppose there would be little need to write this book. We have not. It persists in many ways, and it is difficult to over-estimate the confusion which has entered our thought through this dualism of mind. But of course we cannot blame Plato for it. It was there long before him. In fact not one of us can stand wholly outside this problem and feel that we have entirely solved it. It is because it reaches down to what a modern psychologist has called 'the primary human predicament',[1] that it constitutes the central issue in education. To state this predicament simply we can say that all our lives we have to deal with a world outside and a world inside, and it is because these two worlds are not identical that we find ourselves always striving to understand the relationship between them. Plato in the ninth book of *The Republic*, in which he discusses reality and appearance, is concerned with this predicament. His argument displays a strong fear lest the world of outside things, of tables and chairs, should be destroyed by the inner world of fantasy. He was unable to recognize the close inter-action between them in the design of every-day life.

Indeed it is significant to note that as soon as people begin to think about fact and fantasy they are very soon arguing about goodness and badness. And Plato's fear again was lest free expression of all kinds of feeling should involve a conflict between good

[1] Marion Milner in *On not being able to Paint*, 2nd edition, p. 68.

and bad in which the bad overwhelmed the good. If we allowed this to happen we should be behaving 'like one who gives a city into the hands of villains and destroys the better citizens'. And so he recommended the poets to be purged of all expressions of weakness and violence before they were put into the hands of children. The bad must be driven out and the good preserved.

Many parents and teachers have these fears; as a parent expressed it to me: 'I want to know where self-expression ends, and discipline begins.' I think he was willing to allow for the expression of a certain amount of fantasy in the infant, but then his thought was: 'When can I begin to feel that my child is safe?' He was, of course, probably asking the same question about himself. The poets whom Plato exiled lodged uneasily in his own heart.

These problems concern the educator very closely whatever age he is dealing with, but it is in the nursery and infant schools that they appear most acutely. No teacher watching children in the playground or during free activity time can fail to appreciate the reality of the conflicts in their minds between the real and the unreal, the good and the bad. If these are very severe the child will have to find some way out, because the threat to his personality is too great for him to stand the strain. This is when he becomes very difficult to manage, and is in great need of help. Let us take a close up view of a child in the class room caught in one of these struggles, and let us discover how this particular child tried to deal with it.

I was visiting a poetry lesson in an infant class. The student read two poems, one on a postman and one on a dustman. Then she put the words on the board for the children to copy. But there was a little girl of five who found concentration quite impossible. She came over to me in the corner of the classroom, pushed her paper in front of me and said, 'Do me a "d", I can't do "d's".' I made a row of 'd's in which she was not at all interested, She began to prattle: 'My father is a postman and the other day he put his socks in the dustbin, and do you know the dustman took them out again, and went home with them. How my father laughed.' Once this framework was established, she was able to say what she had to say. There was a pause, such as every artist takes in front of his work, and then very quickly: 'I've got a baby. His name is Douglas: [no wonder she could not do a 'd']. Do you know what my brother did to the baby? [I shake my head and go on making 'd's.] He bit him when my Mother went shopping. He bites me too. I don't bite him, my Daddy says I mustn't.' And so it went on. I repeated the details to the student, who made daily inquiries about the new baby, until one day Millicent burst out, 'We want to get rid of that baby. He cries and keeps Mummy awake, and he does his toilet in his nappies.' In the next free activity time a picture was painted in which there was the typical framework of this age, the blue sky above, green earth below, and the bright yellow cart-wheel sun; inside this was the story. The house occupied the centre of the drawing, on one side of which was a furious scribble, and on the other side was a little rabbit-like creature. She explained that the scribble was Douglas being sent out of the house because he was so naughty, and the good little creature was herself watching him go, ready of course, to enter and take possession.

Millicent had chosen the platonic way out of her predicament. The bad was driven away, and the good preserved and idealized. Plato did not ask where the bad, which he wanted to purge, went to. In this picture we find that it was put upon somebody else. Douglas was blamed for her jealousy. No doubt this opportunity to externalize her feelings in the classroom, which she had sought herself, helped her to lessen the pain of her feelings. But what mattered most was the parental attitude. If she had a mother and father who could understand the inevitability of these feelings and gradually help her to cope with them by sharing the care of the baby, then she would be able to draw a picture where they all lived together in the same house; if it needed to be drawn at all. But unfortunately the world is not full of loving mothers and good educators working together in this way. If it were, it would be a very different place. Even so it is doubtful whether we should entirely avoid 'the primary human predicament'; whether there would ever come a time when what is inside us in our feelings were so harmonized that we developed a full capacity to see the world outside in its true proportion. Yet this is a state towards which we should be tending, and this then is surely the main function of the teacher, not to separate in children the good and the bad, but to allow them both the recognition of each other. In achieving this he will have to allow for the expression of subjective fantasy along with the growing appreciation of external values. But it is easy to appear to do this and yet to be doing something different because we have not fundamentally grasped the significance of the task.

The modern educator cannot escape his doubts and fears through the strong light of conviction in the way that Plato did. Besides there was so much in the Greek way of life that made for balance and sanity. We have inherited a different world, a world of twilight and dawn in which we move about uneasily. Sometimes teachers rush with open arms to embrace progressive methods as a solution of all difficulties without realizing that the closer we are to our fundamental conflicts the more we need to test every inch of the way. With this exuberance often goes a passion for one method above all. Others give lip-service to new ideas and discoveries but their hearts are with the old ways. To such a group belonged the teacher who would not allow a child to draw himself in an aeroplane for 'news' because it was not a fact, but who was prepared to allow the same drawing to be done in a free expression time. But so strong were the immediate feelings of Millicent that there was no escape for her into a world of postman and dustman. She had to break through the whole routine and convention of the lesson to find someone to tell *her* story to. And just as when a little child needs his mother to attend to his wishes, he ceases to regard her as someone who has to cook the dinner for father, so this little girl had no idea of me as a tutor who had come in to watch a lesson, and when I left her to go round the class she gave me a look of anger and fury. Her actions were not divorced from the purpose of the lesson because not until she had coped with her feelings to some extent could she attend to her work at all. And what is a little boy doing when he studies the mechanics of an aeroplane but trying to find out about his own powers of control? How blind we are too if we think that a man's interest in trains which often lasts through life is only an interest in metal and steel and the laws of mechanics. In short, we cannot parcel out our time-table into periods for fact and periods for fantasy and imagine that we have catered for the child's needs, because life is not a pattern of black and white, but an infinitely complex network of differing strands and to a large extent we must leave the child to do his own weaving.

Before then we decide what methods to employ in the classroom let us get a clearer picture of what it is we are allowing children to do. We need to know what a child is freeing himself *from* as well as what he is freeing himself *for*. We need to study release as well as purpose, and what difficult demands these make upon the scheme of a lesson. For the teacher who complains that free activity methods result in licence and lack of discipline is not satisfactorily answered by another who says: 'But in my school I provide plenty of material, organize very carefully and I can stand any amount of noise. Besides everyone is so busily engaged that the question of discipline does not arise.' How often in discussions among teachers is one side pitched against another in this way, and little is gained except that a new kind of jargon is developed. 'Formal' comes to mean 'bad' by the activity teachers, and 'activity' to mean 'bad' by the formal teachers. What is probably being missed by both is the value of conflict, as it is worked out by children inside themselves and in relation to the world outside. To have everybody busily engaged is often very good—very good too, to be able to stand noise and mess; but that does not mean that the teacher can 'liquidate' himself, as I heard it once suggested. No child will be able to come close to these feelings of love and hate and jealousy unless he knows that the teacher is very near.

When we go up to a child who is expressing his inner fantasy in whatever medium, we should neither expect him to stop because we are there; nor to go on as if we were not there. The fact that we are there becomes part of his expression. He asks us to share with him a kind of truth; he wants us to enter his world without losing our position in our own If in a fit of depression he is painting a grey sun in the sky, we should not say: 'I've never seen the sun that colour, and I don't think you have either', neither should we say: 'How wonderful, do you know I think I saw a grey sun the other day.' Both attitudes confuse him. Through us he needs to gain the trust which will enable him to hold two certitudes in his mind at once—one the truth of his sadness, the other the truth of the world which exists in spite of it. As he grows older and becomes more sure of his ability to combine fact and fantasy in his feelings he will relinquish the cart-wheel sun and come to know the one that warms and lights the world. He will become a scientist, but never entirely. There will always remain enough doubt to keep him a poet. And one day perhaps in later life when a cloud passes over the sun, he will feel the chill finger of depression, or when the sun bursts out suddenly, he will give a skip in the middle of the road; and he does not know in such moments how far back he has travelled.

No matter what age we are teaching we are always dealing with both scientists and poets. However far we progress in our knowledge of the physical sciences, we shall also need to provide for that 'willing suspension of disbelief which constitutes poetic faith'.

The best methods educationally will be those where the question of objectivity and subjectivity hardly arises because neither is stressed in allowing for both. But at some moments in the classroom one may assert itself to the apparent exclusion of the other, as fantasy did with Millicent. One can of course be imprisoned in either fact or fantasy. In poetry lessons, children can be lulled through the incantations of verse into complete insensitivity to the poet's meaning; in science lessons, there can be left no room for wonder and 'wild surmise'.

But it is the ability to keep our feelings whole that enables the scientist and the poet to live together within us. The children watching the window cleaner were no doubt satisfying curiosity on many levels. To live fully is to know everything at once, but, as we have seen, if in the act of knowing the painful arises as well as the pleasurable, the jealousy and hatred as well as the love and tenderness, and if we find that these impulses are too much at war for us to keep them together, then it may also be impossible for us to preserve our learning whole. We may have to lose pieces of it by the way. And so the purpose of education is not only to provide means of keeping learning whole as we go along, but also of regaining what has been lost.

The task is no easy one. The child will need plenty of material of all kinds—opportunities for busy activity, and the time too to waste time. But most of all he needs us and our creative understanding. What we say and do as we walk round the room may be more important to some children than what they are doing; to others it may be an interference. We have to watch and judge. We cannot possibly always be right, but a child will go by our intentions, and overlook a clumsy moment, because of the ease he more often experiences in being with us.

But as well as all this, there are times at every age when it is a good thing for him to pack up and listen. The wholesale condemnation of academic learning and so-called formal methods fails to recognize that words are not mere abstractions but symbols for the most primitive parts of our being and that a teacher for whom words are powerful agents can lead a class sitting in their desks to bring their feelings into harmony just as successfully as the one who turns the classroom into a hive of industry. Not only are words potent things, but so are the spaces between them. No good teacher talks all the time, and every lesson moulds itself to the listening qualities of a class as well as to their questions and replies. Bad activity teachers can be very much afraid of this mental space. They grow anxious if a child seems to be left high and dry, and hurriedly move him on. They remind me of the parents of a small boy I once met who kept on asking him: 'Who do you love?', 'Who do you love best?',

'What have you got to give me?' So anxious were they about their child's identity that he was not allowed a moment in which to know himself. Children only realize who and what they are from parents and teachers who know themselves in relation to them.

Moreover whether children are listening or doing, they are always selecting from what they hear and have to do whatever suits their own needs. Millicent picked out of the poetry lesson just what she wanted to symbolize her anxiety and curiosity. She used my advent for her own purpose. She directed me to serve her. She led the student to take note, and she chose paint and paper to say what she had to say. She had an acute problem, and she turned the environment in her direction to help her to solve it. And she did all this because she knew that learning is a means of bringing together the inner and outer aspects of things, a way also of coming to terms with the good and the bad. For we cannot know a thing to be true in fact until we no longer have any need for it to be otherwise.

\*    \*    \*    \*    \*

Plato, like the puritans, is too much afraid of poetic and artistic influences. But he is not without a true sense of the noble purpose to which wit may be applied.

Benjamin Jowett

\*    \*    \*    \*    \*

I could tell myself intellectually that one's dreams are one's own creations, something that one has fashioned out of the vivifying contacts between nature outside and nature within. I could tell myself that we cannot help but dream, completing in imagination the pattern of our necessarily fragmented experience of the external world, we cannot help working over in our imagination what happens to us, creating internally the ideal wholeness of what the experience might have been; just as we continually complete the wholeness of the unseen three sides of a cube and recognize it as a solid in our everyday experience of perceptions. And I could tell myself that without such dreams or expectations of experience re-fashioned out of memory, our lives would be entirely purposeless and blind. But all the same I still caught myself using the phrase 'only imagination'. And I was also at the same time continually caught up in the opposite extreme of so over-valuing the imagination and disparaging the external reality that it was sometimes very difficult to attend to what was going on externally at all. Also although I could tell myself that the inner dream had to be continually tested and enriched by the contact with external reality there still seemed to be difficulty in letting them meet.

Marion Milner
on the difficulties of allowing for the interplay
between dream and external reality

## CHAPTER FIVE

# Exploitation and Exploration

'In a sense I have been writing this all my life. The roots go a long way down; growth has at times been retarded and checked by frosts and storms of circumstance. But in an unobtrusive corner of the mind, the idea has been growing very slowly yet steadily.'

This was how an adult student began the preface to her inquiry into one aspect of Shakespeare's life; and I think it is a good description of how most of our interests work. There is a persistence about them. 'I feel I have laid a ghost' was what another remarked when her study was finished. These mature students admitted to feeling guilty about having a strong interest at all, at their age. Perhaps they thought all their ghosts ought to have been laid. But we can all become very secretive and possessive about our pre-occupations. 'I would not choose my real burning interest', one person said, 'because I don't see why other people should pry into my mind'. More often however we are torn between wanting to share our interests and wanting to keep them to ourselves. This was expressed by the student who, when thanking me for more or less leaving her alone during the year added: 'if you had interfered and tried to make it go your way, I should have felt like murder. Now I don't mind who reads it.'

Yet none of this is very surprising when we recollect that there is nothing new under the sun; and that the unsatisfied curiosities and unquietened fears of our childhood go their hungry, stealthy ways throughout our lives; that the friendships we make, the social groups to which we belong, the jobs we choose (if we are lucky enough to choose), the books we read, and all the other interests we follow are in part the pursuit of lovers and the pursuits of ghosts. So when we talk about interest in education, which we do a great deal nowadays, let us make sure that we have no patched up affair, no artificial imposition, but the 'mad pursuit' and 'the wild ecstasy' which all learning sets going.

In fact, whenever an interest is aroused we move both forward and backward: backward to pick up our old loves and fears; forward in the realm of facts and other people's experience; and this mobility is a sign of learning health. But that does not mean that we must keep moving for fear of standing still. There are times in learning when we seem to be getting nowhere at all, a kind of necessary stage of bewilderment. This state can be very painful indeed. We can feel like someone caught in revolving doors seeing the way back and the way forward, and yet not going one way or the other. But often these doors connect our different ways of knowing, and what seems like confusion and uncertainty is a movement in the process of clarification.

This confusion stage reminds me of Peer Gynt's meeting with the Boyg in Ibsen's play. When Peer came to the dark hill where the Boyg lived, he felt he did not know where nor who he was; and so he began to slash and beat about. But whenever he demanded that a way should be made clear for him, he always received the same reply:

Go round about Peer, the hill's roomy enough.

The root idea of this Norwegian word 'boyg' is sinuous, bending, which certainly gives the lie to the interpretation sometimes given of this scene, that it represents the spirit of compromise. The Boyg admits no compromise but he is nevertheless complete master of a roundabout situation. And when at every point Peer expects to be given battle and finds only that he is met by this paradoxical creature he is confused and distressed. We can sense the revolving doors situation in the lines:

Forward and back, and it's just as far;
Out or in, and it's just as straight.

He is *there*! and *there*! And he's round the bend.
No sooner I'm out than I'm back in the ring.
Name who you are! Let me see you. What are you?

To this question the Boyg has always the same uncompromising reply:

Myself. Can you say the same?

We can only escape these states of bewilderment as ourselves if we can stand the distress of having to look in several directions; to go roundabout and yet still make our way along. No wonder, in order to avoid this pain, we have in the last few generations become so obsessed with the idea of progress as something which is continual movement forward. But true progress is not like this; and in order to find out what it is we must have room enough in which to get lost. It becomes the teacher's concern to make this room, and also to develop a sinuous quality of direction.

For five years I was in close contact with a scheme of individual studies for adult students to which I have already made reference.[1] They were asked to choose any topic in which they were deeply interested and to follow it for a year wherever it led them. The tutor's function in relation to these studies had a 'boyg' quality, because however much the study veered in this or that direction, often changing its title many times, and sometimes its topic, she tried to remain bending and quiescent; to guide without direction and to suggest without prescription. But very few students escaped the painful stages of bewilderment and the diaries in which they recorded the progress of their work reflected the whirl of ideas in which they were caught from time to time, particularly just before a new piece of understanding was reached. This they came to suffer because they found that the onslaught tactics availed very little. I think that the majority of

[1] This experiment was made at Borthwick Women's Emergency Training College—1946–1951.

them would have found Peer Gynt's outcry an echo of their state of mind, because they came to see that the pursuit of a genuine interest is a method of self-discovery.

The best of these investigations from the onlooker's point of view (they were not all verbally presented), were those in which the need to express and know themselves kept time in the students with the acquisition of facts and ideas. The worst were those where the energy driving towards discovery was so strong that it overwhelmed the ideas, or where the fear to follow an interest was so great that it caused them to seek refuge in the accumulation of facts. They dared not risk the revolving process of clarification. Such students were of course learning-ill; they had not enough grasp of their own identity to yield to the sinuous quality of interest. No wonder that these studies gave us the best single measure of a student's capabilities and personality development that we had discovered.

However, we recognized as the work went on that not only was it necessary, in order to preserve a learning health, for the acquisition of knowledge to keep pace with the inner curiosity, but that they were interdependent. In fact I was often reminded of Dryden's reply to the question whether poetry should please or instruct. 'It instructs as it pleases.' There it is in a nutshell. We cannot go out as explorers of reality until we have exploited it to some extent and yet we explore as we exploit, and often vice-versa. Watch the baby who, when he has exploited his mother's body for food and warmth, begins to explore it with his hands and mouth. He pulls her hair, pokes her eyes, kisses her one minute, pinches her the next, and allows himself this orgy of discovery because he is aware of her capacity to feed and love him. So a child learns, and the degree of his success in this learning will be in direct relation to his primary satisfactions and frustrations. To alleviate the pain of not having, and to repeat our moments of satisfaction are both incentives to learning. A teacher's success, therefore, is measured not only by his ability to widen a child's horizons but also by his skill in leading him back to regain his lost provinces, to recapture his old delights. We might put it another way and say that our horizons only become clear as the work of consolidation of gains and replacement of losses takes place.

Perhaps at this moment the teacher is ready to protest that a class moving in several directions presents too much confusion to be coped with. In fact this fear is generally behind the criticism that activity methods make for licence. By a strict control of the lesson and a rigid dictation of work, the teacher often labours under the illusion that he has these conflicting tendencies in check. Fortunately the mind is a freer agent than he thinks, and there are sometimes windows to look through, pages to doodle upon, and even behind the alert, attentive look a child can train his mind to wander. If we do not allow him a true mobility of mind, he will have to produce a false one through rebellion and cussedness. But whatever the attitude of the teacher, there will be days when, like Peer, some children seem to be fighting with darkness and unknown voices. They appear cantankerous, peevish or perhaps develop a physical symptom. They may be clumsy and upset things by accident. Here again we need the Boyg's response; and the more the child finds that we can stand his groping attacks, the sooner will he realize that there is room enough for him after all and get on with things.

There is, I have found, little difference fundamentally between the way children and adults pursue their interests, because in order to regain lost provinces, the grown-up will have to regress to childhood to some extent, whilst the child is in many ways exceedingly mature. We are all teachers and learners together but not in any sentimental way in which sometimes adults pretend to be like children, but out of a very real and urgent human need to share what the world offers. What as teachers we are concerned with is not so much to protect the sources of ideas, as to ensure that an interest is flexible enough to allow teachers and taught to go round about.

However, I cannot imagine anything less likely to arouse the personal sources of interest than the false impositions which so often masquerade as local and social studies. Let this not stand as a condemnation of these methods when they are taught so that they are the fruit of genuine inquiry, but because his interests sometimes run in the direction of local place-names, the coal industry, food distribution and so on, it does not mean that every child will be absorbed in these things for the same length of time. The centre of interest has one great advantage over the subject curriculum. It can often be more roomy. But not necessarily. Every subject has vast sources of interest if taught properly, whilst a centre of interest mismanaged can be more impaling than anything. A child can be encouraged to fritter away his energies in the service of what looks like a communal effort, when in fact it is a welding together of bits of interest often spasmodically invoked to fulfil the teacher's aim of producing a good citizen. But a child can only become a good citizen in as far as he is a whole and integrated person and that integration comes from the deep emotional levels we have been considering; it does not arise from artificially constructed schemes.

Let us spread rich wares from many markets before children and watch where the eye glitters. Of course any method of teaching can become a mystique and teachers do not easily relinquish the idea that there is an inner shrine of learning to which they alone hold the key. I was caught up in this mystique thinking whilst arranging this book, for I was exercised in my mind about which chapter would fall in the middle of the seven. Would it be the core chapter, the centre and heart of it all?

\*     \*     \*     \*     \*

We all of us fancy we must have a core at the centre, . . . we would like to hold within us some specially dainty kernel, or nut, protecting the future, the everlasting. And we do not realize, cannot realize that we have in fact no kernel but are made up of one leaf on top of another from outermost to innermost, that in fact we are onions.

> Georg Groddeck in *Exploring the Unconscious*.
> He is following the ruminations of Peer Gynt
> peeling an onion.

## CHAPTER SIX

# Confidence and Diffidence

Dr Johnson thought that the *Elegy Written in a Country Churchyard* was justly admired because, as he put it, it abounded 'with images which find a mirror in every mind and with sentiments to which every bosom returns an echo'. I think it is easy to understand why this poem appealed so strongly to a man who in his own personality revealed such a complex mixture of pride and humility, dogmatism and fear, for this is the main subject of the elegy. It reaches down through many levels of understanding to the confidence and diffidence which are essential aspects of human nature. Through the exquisite plaint of the poem runs the theme which is in one of its renderings also a theme of tragedy: the waste of sweetness and the loss of good.

> Full many a gem of purest ray serene
> The dark unfathom'd caves of ocean bear;
> Full many a flower is born to blush unseen
> And waste its sweetness on the desert air.

It is against this waste that education wages a ceaseless war, for one of its chief aims is to give children the opportunity to come into their own. But perhaps if we realized more imaginatively the delicacy of the task we should try to discover finer tools with which to carry it out.

Nowhere does the fundamental lack of confidence show itself more clearly than where the question of self-expression crops up. I was brought very closely into touch with the intricacies of the situations involved in such work when conducting classes in original writing. I realized that grown-ups and children have to face similar difficulties and that it is perhaps easier to study the issues involved where the former are concerned; so I will describe some of my findings from the class among the adult students referred to in the last chapter.

It was a voluntary group in which there was plenty of room for manœuvre. Work was given in when and how the students liked. They could be in spate for a season and then dry up or contribute regularly. They could follow suggestions from the classes or find their own themes. They could write prose or verse. The group itself was spacious in that the age range was very wide (about 21–45 years); the students were married and unmarried, with and without children. Some had experience in writing, others had not written in any creative sense since they were at school, if then. On the whole there was much more diffidence than confidence in the group. My chief problem was to discover how 'to break up a long-continued frost'.

At first many defences and disguises were adopted. These were mainly of a literary kind. One student wrote Miltonics, another imitated eighteenth-century pedantries, another adopted journalese and so on. I now see how significant these masks were, and also how painful and slow in some cases was the losing of them. When they found that their efforts were not meeting with my full appreciation, they began to ask: 'What is wrong with my style?', or 'What is wrong with your judgement?' After this stage was reached the questions changed to 'Why haven't I got anything original to say?', or 'Why don't you like what I have to say?' Then two kinds of expression came to the surface—a bevy of apologies, and several outbursts of frustration. Some responded by shrinking from the task of self-expression; others made excuses for their inadequacies by blaming circumstances; or felt that the demands of everyday life prevented them from getting into touch with themselves.[1]

[1] In the original edition examples of 'apology' poems, etc., were given. These are omitted here. There were too few to carry the complexity of the ideas arising. Further, so significant did I subsequently find this work that I went on to research in it. An account of this research is at present being written under the title *The Articulate Self*.

My main problem was how to show the students that until they had taken a look at all sides of themselves they would not be able to say what they wanted. I tried a little prodding. I suggested that 'beautiful' in the artistic sense was not the same as the more popular use of the word. A poet could describe 'garbage' and produce something beautiful. I read Spenser's description of the revolting dragon in the den of error, and proclaimed it a beautiful passage. Some agreed, some were mystified, others outraged. Then a few 'garbage' poems appeared and quotations from the poets in this kind. I knew however that this intellectual approach could only touch the surface. They needed some kind of sanction to come closer to those earlier frustrations which lay at the root of their inarticulateness. Then I read two essays on quite different levels of self-revelation —Abraham Cowley's *Of Myself* and D. H. Lawrence's on *Thinking about Oneself*. The ice cracked more loudly than I had anticipated, and it was Lawrence's passage about the skeletons that did it.

> It is perfectly natural for every man and every woman to think about himself or herself most of the time. What is there to be afraid of? And yet people as a mass are afraid. You'd think everybody had a skeleton in the cupboard of their inside. Which of course they have. I've got a skeleton, and so have you. But what's wrong with him . . . if he wants to have a chat with me, let him.

This was taken as my request for their skeletons. Lawrence escaped most of the blame. Then came a few protests:

> Each one of us is only supremely important to himself, and his entirely personal outpourings seldom satisfy the needs of others. By all means when the grief and disturbance is rampant let it be tamed by a timely utterance; but as there are other sources of inspiration than the need to fetter tigers, we do not need to summon real or imaginary beasts from a real or imaginary jungle in order to write.
> Permit us please to let sleeping skeletons lie.

I remarked on how much I had enjoyed her protest, and that it was the most vigorous piece of writing she had given in so far. In most cases however there was less resistance than relief, and I noticed more ease and sincerity in the writing after this.

However, it became clear to me that the question of confidence and diffidence where creative work was concerned was far more complex than I had imagined—so many aspects of human nature were involved.

At the outset most of the students decided that they would rather remain anonymous when their work was read and discussed. If they did not want it to be made public at all, they wrote to that effect on the top. But slowly as their confidence in me and in each other grew, this diffidence almost disappeared. One piece of intimate autobiographical writing was given in which I praised very highly, but remarked that the student would probably not want me to read it out as its anonymity was unlikely to be preserved. I was astounded at her complete surrender when she remarked: 'If you like it as much as that I don't mind.' This was a turning point in the development of her work.

So it became clear that secrecy and diffidence were closely connected with approval and disapproval. But why were these grown-up women, who were most of them running homes and rearing families, still so dependent upon the glance of the tutor? When at the end of the year a selection of the work was put out on 'open day', a few of them wanted to withdraw their contributions in case their husbands and families saw them. A kind of safety zone had been constructed at the college, which however did not extend in every case to their own homes. They had not yet gained the courage which every artist needs when he turns his products into the world. But our sternest critics are the parental voices which so often remain inside us, and we are inclined to invest the people around us with these judging roles, which does not of course mean that those people are always innocent of assuming them. How well in the light of all this one can understand the mixture of trepidation and delight which most children feel when they bring their parents to school to see what they have done, and in their glances of anxious expectation one can discern that point of balance between advance and retreat which is so momentous for the development of our trust in the world.

The students had placed me also in a parental role. I decided at the beginning of the course to throw my efforts in with the rest to come up for criticism. But I found that I had made a mistake. I discussed the matter with them and they agreed that it was better for me to keep out. It helped them to know that I could write; it was also a good thing for them to realize that there were better writers in the group; but whilst they were creating they felt they needed the illusion of my invulnerability.

And yet I could also see that it was not wise for me to take the role of a judge entirely. In any case this was impossible as my own unconscious attitudes were bound to operate in my criticism, and these the students had every right to challenge. I found it easier to give scope for this challenge in relation to my criticism than in relation to my own creative efforts and apparently the students also felt the one attack more permissible than the other. I think it likely that with more experience of this kind of work, it would have become possible to break down some of these resistances on both sides. All this opens up an extremely important aspect of the teacher–child relationship, which it is not possible to go into here, but I would put forward the suggestion that both the students and myself were probably reflecting an important stage in our early reactions to our parents, where we found it disturbing to question their uniqueness and yet at the same time were bound to rebel against their judgements, especially when we had other and perhaps better standards before us. It seems necessary therefore for the teacher to adopt a method whereby he can allow for a notion of infallibility and at the same time give space for rebellion against it. But as soon as the children can come into their own expression, the conflict will be to a large extent solved, and the disguises and subterfuges can drop away.

Another interesting point from this class, which can only be touched upon now arose in relation to 'style'. After the students lost the suits and trappings which they had adopted (some of these had been encouraged at school), they used all manner of loose forms as well as following stricter patterns of verse. They saw that style and meaning were inevitably linked, and they respected the author who said, 'What I have written, I have written', even though they indulged in some tinkering here and there. Expression is a forcing outwards into the light of recognition not only our most satisfying achievements but the agonies and inadequacies which are part of them. We shall have to re-write many of our aesthetic theories when we come more thoroughly to understand that form itself is as much unconsciously motivated as are the meanings which it enfolds. But this points to a most fascinating line of enquiry out of the scope of this essay.

What I felt had emerged most clearly from this class was that the building up of confidence in expression was very closely connected with the coming to terms with guilt in the personality. If we are not sure what will come out if we express ourselves freely, then we are likely to find ways of concealing what is there; and so we go through our lives avoiding the realities which give us life. How well Viola understood the dangers of this concealment as well as the pain of reserve.

VIOLA: My father had a daughter loved a man,
As it might be perhaps were I a woman
I should your lordship.

DUKE: And what's her history?

VIOLA: A blank my lord. She never told her love.
But let concealment, like a worm i' the bud,
Feed on her damask cheek: she pined in thought;
And, with a green and yellow melancholy,
She sat like patience on a monument,
Smiling at grief. Was this not love indeed?

DUKE: But died thy sister of her love my boy?

VIOLA: I am all the daughters of my fathers' house
And all the brothers too:—and yet I know not.

Now let us discover what we have learnt from all this which can be applied as an educational principle. We saw that some students could express themselves fairly easily; what they wanted was the opportunity; with others a more tortuous route was necessary. Defences had to be broken down, and I had to exercise a double function. I had to provide the class with material to study, and at the same time to give a moral sanction. It meant giving the good things of literature, but not minding at first what was given in return. It meant showing that true expression only results from a fearless attitude towards what is inside one. The authentic poem or essay is the one in which concealment is not necessary because what had to be concealed has become part of what has to be revealed. This does not mean that expression is nothing but the letting of skeletons out of cupboards. When we know what is in a room, cupboards and all, we can give our attention to living in it as we want to. If we have to keep an eye all the time on some part of it to control what might be there, then what we want to say is perpetually under the influence of what we dare not say. To begin with, before our courage has fully developed it is a great help if there is somebody else in the room to help with the situation.

Children's original work is strengthened by the quality and freedom of the discussion that takes place in a classroom no matter what the subject involved and so long as the teacher respects the advance and retreat that characterizes good discussion in general. At one time diffidence must be given the benefit of confidence, at another confidence of diffidence. In all this we are re-enacting for the child what happened to him at a much earlier age when the quality of his courage was first developed. The parents are the child's first audience and he finds his feet in time to their loving glances, their imaginative sympathy with his gains and losses. The baby soon learns to scan his mother's face to find in the creases and furrows there, in the changing lights in her eyes, where his own value lies. At one moment perhaps he turns to her with passionate desire to possess her love entirely, and she may thoughtlessly turn away or bring an impatient note into the voice, because the door-bell rang or there were so many things waiting to be done. At such times a child may become depressed, for he may think that it was his greed and desire that caused her to turn away. Here both parents and teachers will no doubt show some impatience and exclaim: 'Then we had better give it up. The home and school make too many demands upon us to allow us to respond to such acute sensitivity.' But we do not alter the facts of feeling because we have developed a feeling for fact. We have to weld them together as best we can. The good mother in attending to her baby's emotional needs learns to create a safety zone round herself in which the child can show both his daring and his hesitancy; a place where there is room for advance and retreat to find their own rhythm. Then gradually he will be able to allow her to go away or to rebuke him and still feel that his expression has not been damaged. He will begin to play games of bo-peep with her, he will laugh when she frowns and frown when she laughs just to prove that he has gained enough confidence in the world to test it out in sport. So much of our learning in later life is built upon these patterns, and the teacher, too, needs to create zones of safety.

The glance of the teacher then and the mother must show the child that he is acceptable; but also it must allow for the exposure of the greedy worm if the sweetness is to be divulged and the reserve broken down. Good mothers and good teachers have always known this. It is only because we so often fail in our upbringing of children that we have to formulate our intuitions. But—

> He who can open the bud does it so simply.
> He gives it a glance, and the life sap stirs through its veins.
> At his breath, the flower spreads its wings and flutters in the wind.
> Colours flush out like heart-longings, the perfume betrays a sweet secret.
> He who can open the bud does it so simply.[1]

Rabindranath Tagore—*Fruit-Gathering*, No. XVIII.

I think we need to learn in education how to recapture sim-
plicity. Civilization and the complexities of modern life have
made natural methods of child rearing more difficult. Schools
are in any case artificial places. Now it is our task to cultivate
what was once taken for granted; but the cultivated plant need
not be forced; it can still take the soil and feel the air and warmth
the same as its more wayward brother, and the loss of profusion
can be compensated for by careful pruning, so long as we keep
in mind how many varieties there are.

Although Gray's 'Elegy' was only briefly referred to at the
beginning of this chapter its main themes have been reverber-
ating throughout. It is not an easy poem to come to grips with;
one can lose the strong vibrations within the verses and the
powerful cross-currents if too much attention is paid to the
prose meaning and to the literary and historical allusions—
important though these are. William Empson, for instance is so
anxious to guard against being tricked by the poet into thinking
that man is better off by living within his limitations and
without cultural opportunities that he fails to notice the essential
ambivalence of the whole poem. He brushes aside the famous
fourteenth stanza with the commonsense conclusion that a
gem does not mind being in a cave and a flower prefers not to be
picked. He disliked the smug, puritanical sentiments of the poem
—the sexual suggestion in the phrase 'to blush unseen' implied
he complained that virginity was in itself a good thing, and that
so was any renunciation.[1] All this is fair comment so far but
fails to take into account Gray's attempt to explore both sides of
human nature—the jocund *and* the melancholy, the fecund *and*
the infecund, and so on. We can at this distance only guess what
it was in the poem to have caused General Wolfe to declaim it
to his officers on the eve of the battle of Quebec, and to have

---

[1] These remarks from Empson are discussed in the excellent commentary
on 'the Elegy' to be found in Chapter 6 of *The Well Wrought Urn*, by Cleanth
Brooks, pp. 102–3.

added, 'I would prefer being the author of that poem to the glory of beating the French tomorrow.' Most likely he was referring to the subtle ironies of the poem where pride and modesty are cunningly related as they are so often in the soldier; whilst the couplet which oddly enough has baffled so many critics could not fail in its passionate protest to stir the hearts of men on the eve of battle:

> E'en from the tomb the voice of nature cries,
> E'en in our ashes live their wonted fires.

How swiftly Gray turns from this expression of sublime tenacity to the wayward fancies of the melancholy poet and to the conclusion that hope is at best a precarious adjustment.

> No farther seek his merits to disclose,
> Or draw his frailties from their dread abode,
> (There they alike in trembling hope repose)
> The bosom of his Father and his God.

With less piety but more poetic faith Shelley has written of 'the fading coal' of inspiration and in another place of its 'unextinguished hearth'. He has given us the poet in his most exalted mood and in his most vulnerable hour. Learning takes place within the extremes of triumph and despair, varying in concentration from moment to moment.

\*    \*    \*    \*    \*

> Drive my dead thoughts over the universe,
> Like withered leaves, to quicken a new birth;
> And by the incantation of this verse,
> Scatter, as from an unextinguished hearth
> Ashes and sparks, my words among mankind!
> Be through my lips to unawakened earth
> The trumpet of a prophecy! O wind,
> If winter comes, can Spring be far behind?

Percy Bysshe Shelley
*Ode to the West Wind*

The mind in creation is as a fading coal, which some invisible influence, like an inconstant wind, awakens to transitory brightness; this power rises from within like the colour of a flower which fades and changes as it is developed; and the conscious portions of our nature are unprophetic either of its approach or its departure. Could this influence be durable in its original purity and force, it is impossible to predict the greatness of the results; but when composition begins, inspiration is already on the decline, and the most glorious poetry that has ever been communicated to the world is probably a feeble shadow of the original conceptions of the poet.

*A Defence of Poetry*
Percy Bysshe Shelley

# CHAPTER SEVEN

# Principle and Prejudice

As I look back upon these essays it seems as though I had invited the reader into a junk shop. What an oddly assorted group of people are here: Viola making common cause with Gray's melancholy poet; the sardonic and unprepossessing Socrates consorting with delicate Ariel; dragons, ghosts and skeletons brushing against the fragrant rose of the Indian poet; and Plato sacrilegiously compared to a window cleaner. I feel sure that readers will say that I am using the gems of literature very badly by taking them out of their fine and original settings and flinging them into this medley assortment. But so steadfast in their own intentions are the great masters that I do not think that my delinquencies will disturb them. I did not of course deliberately bring these creatures together, it was the paradox in my mind that caused this junk shop to appear. But the birth of a paradox is nearly always a little painful. It is painful to have to look at the ugly as well as the perfect so that beauty can arise; to look at destruction along with the ideal, before we can know what is good; to fall into error before we can reach the truth. How much easier it is to raise these words—truth, beauty and goodness—like so many monuments, without acknowledging the worm in the bud which they conceal, and the grief which they avoid. We have lived far too long in education at the feet of these pedestalled values.

I have stressed the importance of so many things we have been taught to avoid; chaos, muddle, conflict, depression, rebellion, incoherence, fantasy, getting lost, looking for skeletons and all manner of distressing things. In fact I have asserted the value of illness. But we have discovered that illness can best be described relatively. There may be a stage in learning when to realize difficulties is most beneficial to progress, but sometimes these may have gone too far for us to be able thus to turn them to account. And this can happen sometimes to the best material there is. Was there a nobler mind than Hamlet's to be over-thrown?

Some of the things which troubled Hamlet were not unlike those which caused distress to the little girl, Millicent.[1] We saw how she was dividing her picture in two because she could not bear to look at herself as a whole; how she put the bad in one half and the good in the other, and identified herself with the good. This is just what Hamlet did when he compared his father with his uncle:

'First look upon this picture, and on this.'

and how the passionate prejudice of his language betrayed the under-lying jealousy. It becomes an important part of the teacher's task to recognize these things and to try to keep learning whole by helping the child to catch up with different sides of himself. Or as I rhymed it for myself:

The black and the white
Weave them together
Through darkness and light
In foul and fair weather.

Keep the thief on the run
And where find the lover?
But overtake one,
You'll pick up the other.

I am wondering whether the nervous exhaustion which teachers so frequently suffer from is not closely connected with the efforts they feel bound to make in order to keep children up

[1] See p. 29.

to their own very high standards. They rarely notice how unsuccessful they are in any long-term sense. They are following the platonic lead and expecting the bad to disappear in some miraculous way, the more they put the accent on the good. But it does not work like that. After one of the familiar moral exhortations from the platform by the head teacher, things can seem quite different for a time. Behaviour improves and the general tone of the school is uplifted. Everything is cleaned up, and everyone is exalted. But not for long, unless real creative love is at work, and a tolerance which touches the roots of human nature and is prepared to take it for what it is. Here the teacher is no doubt ready to explain that surely he is not there to encourage wrong-doing and naughtiness. But the sources of these things are not under his control as much as he thinks, nor are they likely to get out of his control as much as he fears. Difficult children in class are difficult, and to try by disciplinary measures to hide this does not in any way alter the situation. But this does not mean that no discipline should be used. What matters is how we use it. Do we control the child because we are afraid of what will result if we do not— are we trying to suppress inner badness? Or do we control him because we know that close to the heart of that badness lies the value he has for the world, and our control is the expression of the love that recognizes this?

The inability to distinguish between these two kinds of discipline leads to much confusion of thought and practice which shows itself very clearly in the attitude which sections of the general public take towards maladjustment. Modern educators are blamed for letting children do what they like, and psychologists, it is thought, are their aiders and abettors. Unfortunately there is enough bad education going on under progressive banners, and a large enough number of misguided psychologists for these accusers to find the culprit they so desperately need. But the teachers who base their methods upon psychological principles, clinically tested, know much better than their arraigners that it is disastrous to let a child do just what he likes, and so does the teacher who has never heard of psychology, but who works from the love that is in him; because they know that pleasure and pain are inseparable in rich and courageous living. This, however, is a very different thing from saying, as some magistrates and others have been known to say, that pain is good for a child. Let these magistrates recall their own misdeeds and realize that the children before them differ from themselves chiefly in the *measure* of their difficulties; and let them look for causes not in the school alone, a handy and easy scapegoat, but in the complex structure of human nature and society, which it should be their humble and patient task to study.

As well as in the school, the cause for delinquency is sought in the bad conditions of the home, and in the unhappy relationship of parents. This is nearer to the heart of the matter. But it should be realized that a child gets beyond parental control in one sense as soon as he casts doubt upon his parents' love, and this can happen very early in his life and in homes where everything on the surface seems all right. Nor is it easy to blame parents for actions which they themselves are unaware of committing—nor for an inability to respond to the acute sensibilities of children, which their own upbringing may have blinded them to.

It was with such thoughts in mind that I looked again at some of our educational methods. I have suggested that *activity* is an indispensable technique if it allows the balance of forces in a child so to be felt, that by getting to know himself, other people and the outside world gain in value for him. But we have to realize that this principle underlies all good teaching of whatever kind, listening, writing, speaking, acting, moving and so on. We must be careful not to set up an altar to something called *activity*, and imagine that any other method is under suspicion, without testing the principles upon which all of them are based.

So it is with *interest*. We have learnt to understand through psychology a good deal about children's interests, but little that inspired teachers have not always known. But in talking of 'the child's need', we must realize that this is not the same thing as 'Mary Brown's need'. This latter is something we can begin to guess at from her behaviour over a long period, but never really know. Only she knows where her genuine interests lie. We can cater for what they are likely to be; but to do this knowing our limitations is a very different thing from planning with a false belief in our powers of prophecy. This places us in a difficult position. We have to plan for the unknown and yet know something about what we plan for. No wonder teachers who lack the necessary flexibility for such methods bring them into disrepute. Because what we are really saying is that every lesson should be a creative act, and this is something that both activity and interest teachers often overlook. They know that material must be produced for the child's mind to act upon, but they often fail to realize that children also construct within themselves material upon which they act.

This creative aspect of education is the one which in all the centuries of our civilization has been most neglected. At last, however, the recognition of its importance is growing. But courage is needed here from the teacher, because it is not an easy thing to leave children face to face with their own chaos. This means being prepared to receive distortions of reality and incoherence of many kinds before there gradually emerge satisfying shapes and forms. Appreciation and making things from directions are both valuable activities because we learn much through identification and emulation, but to fashion something right out of ourselves is a much more satisfying thing to do. I wonder whether to submit a child thus to the hazards of creation is not the best educational opportunity that we can offer him. Further we should not overlook the extent to which the theory of education can become an escape from creativity; and much also that goes under the name of appreciation. Learning provides us with many ways of vicarious living, and it is often difficult to know whether we are cheating or not. For example to read in Virgil of Aeneas' grief over all the dead of the Trojan War may provide an experience of different kinds; we may recognize our own griefs and so come to understand 'sunt lacrimae rerum, et mentem mortalia tangunt'. ('There are tears for events and mortal sorrows touch the heart.') No one would doubt that this is an experience of great value, but there is a way of weeping Aeneas' tears in order to escape from our own which perhaps we fear, if we gave place to them, might shatter all our being. But not until we can endure the full extent of our own suffering will the 'lacrimae rerum' be of much creative value to humanity.

Are there then no standards outside ourselves? Must we reach all our principles through the dangerous mazes of prejudice? What is there that we can be sure of? I have tried to show in these essays that one of our educational aims is that we should come to recognize our prejudices and illusions so that we are in a better position to test out reality. But we have seen also that owing to the great complexity of the task for most of us, all we can hope for is an approximation to this aim; whereas the more we try to invoke certainty, the more we shall retard even this approximation.

When I was engaged upon the work in individual studies already referred to,[1] I was struck by the attitudes of the many different people to whom the students applied for help. The response they met with on all sides was extremely generous, because I think the sincerity of the purpose was recognized; but sometimes they came upon the fear, especially among the more learned bodies, that these studies would be inaccurate and lack standard if approached from such a subjective angle. In fact the finished products varied as much as the students. But there were even among these bodies those who recognized that the standard was inherent in the work itself. This is surely what scholarship is—an insatiable demand for the satisfaction of curiosity by means of a patient sifting of evidence, and when in this process meaning seems to dawn, it comes with the light of revelation, because we recognize both what we have always known, and what we have just come to find out. But I think that we must recognize the scholarship which cannot allow for error and wrong judgement to be in itself a defensive structure.

[1] See pp. 36–9.

It is for the teacher to ensure that the achievements of learning bring to the child advancement and culture but also he should allow him to use them as so much raw material with which to begin all over again: for were they not achieved as the result of conflicts and satisfactions similar to his own?

\*     \*     \*     \*     \*

It is impossible to produce scholars, who in the true sense of the word are wise men, if they know nothing about themselves.

Lawrence S. Kubie

\*     \*     \*     \*     \*

In spite of Hegel, the Victorians were not a dialectically minded age; they did not think naturally in opposites, of positives and negatives as aspects of the same whole. Paradoxes troubled rather than pleased them. They were not the people for existentialist moments, but for chains of cause and effect, for positive all-explaining theories, carefully studied and studiously applied.

> John Fowles in *The French Lieutenant's Woman*, 'An allegory on the decline of the static Victorian ethos and on the birth of the twentieth-century passion for freedom.'

# PART TWO

## On Guidance

### On the nature of true guidance

Sometimes he would be using two approaches at the same time, playful yet not so playful, artless yet full of art. . . . He was a master of prepared improvisation and studied offhandedness, and to adapt another theatrical saying, 'threw his lines away' among the boys in such a manner that they were quite certain to be picked up. He qualified almost everything that sounded like crystallised definition, thus uncrystallising it. . . . He approached the boys himself with so little weight of preconception. He did not await confirmation of some pattern formed about them in his mind, although his long training had made him familiar with many patterns; nor did there intervene between him and them any picture of what he wanted them to be or thought they ought to be or might be. He remained entirely open to receive the impressions of them as they were, entire.

Michael Burn

On George Lyward. From
*Mr Lyward's Answer*

## CHAPTER EIGHT

# Reflections on the Teacher's Need for Guidance[1]

I do not want to set up as an arbiter between inspectors and teachers, but rather to try to look at some of the things which teachers think and feel about their own needs. At the same time these cannot be thought of out of relation to the people who try to satisfy them. We now know too much about human nature to think that impartiality can ever be completely attained in relation to another person or ourselves. Perhaps it is as difficult to be impartial in our judgement of teachers as it is of parents. Whatever is said about them is said by someone who has been taught.

Teachers are more consciously seeking help than they ever did before, and that makes the task of co-operation easier. A teacher wrote to me the other day in answer to an enquiry I was asked to make into the frustrations and satisfactions of the teacher's job, and, under the heading of inspectors (he found his own headings), he wrote: 'Their approach to the practising teacher would appear at the present time to be ideal. This spirit of co-operation and enquiry must be fostered.' One wonders whether that could have been written fifty or even twenty years ago. It has taken us a long time to realize that authority can be maintained along with co-operation, and to admit that there is no place in education for onlookers and overseers.

[1] This paper was delivered to an international conference for Inspectors organized by the New Education Fellowship, Chichester, April 1955. It was published in *The New Era*, June 1955, pp. 107–112.

Inspectors by definition are not lookers-on, but lookers into, and the Oxford dictionary explains that the word 'look' comprises two meanings: examination and contemplation. This is how teachers like to feel they are being guided, with a mind that is both analytic and synthetic. I do not think they want familiarity or over-enthusiasm, or a hail-fellow-well-met attitude. Teachers stand in real need of someone whom they can respect and look up to, and at the same time talk with on a professional level as equals. Sometimes a headmaster serves this purpose —but not in quite the way in which an inspector can, if he will take the role of itinerant philosopher.

What an extraordinary place a classroom is. Headmasters and headmistresses come in and out, colleagues, and sometimes children from other classes, visitors occasionally; but most of the time the teacher rules his kingdom alone; and within the framework of those four walls a strange life takes place, where triumph and defeat, loyalty and enmity, boredom and revelation and many contrasted feelings come and go. Different relationships are worked out, whilst the retreats from contact are just as significant. The aspects of the teacher which the children never know directly will be felt. Indirectly learning gains its impulse from a complex emotional life—of which, much of the time, neither teacher nor child is fully aware. A classroom is a very safe place once a working understanding between a teacher and his class has been established. It may very easily become far too safe. The best classroom is one where reticence is respected but curiosity is kept on the move. When anyone comes in to watch a lesson this pattern is bound to be disturbed. Children look at teachers in a new way when teachers are being looked at. Teachers alter their focus when children are being observed through themselves. The more one compares the classroom situation with any other circumstances in life, the more curious does it appear. We take it for granted because we have all spent years and years in classrooms.

One of the functions of inspectors is to focus the classroom for the teacher who cannot easily do this for himself. He is in it as part of the picture. He needs an artist from the outside: someone who will bring with him a sensitive mind, resonant, expectant—listening with the third ear to the tones and undertones of the lesson, watching the light and dark, and all the shapes and forms it takes; allowing appraisal and criticism to point and outline and crispen—illuminating not as in a court of law, but in a place where mysteries are shared. Then afterwards let the artist-observer describe what he has seen and felt. The teacher may not agree with all that is said; indeed it may be as much off the mark as on it. It will hardly matter at this stage. The value for the teacher lies in the fact that someone has cared about him in this way—has given him definition. I am not suggesting that this is all that is required of those who go into lessons, but I think it is a necessary preparatory stage—a stage of recognition and definition. It gives the teacher a sense of identity which it is not easy to gain in a classroom, indeed which it is perilously easy to lose.

Teachers are much concerned with the sense of identity. They gain it very largely through the method they use in teaching. On this they like to put their stamp so that it shall be recognized in the results. They rejoice of course when individuality is preserved, but they look nevertheless for the mark which is themselves. This distinguishing mark of the teacher is a baffling phenomenon. It is like a family resemblance—subtle, indelible.

What seems to cause the deepest resentment in teachers is the suggestion that they should adopt methods with which they are out of sympathy. The young teacher who spoke of the co-operation between inspectors and teachers wrote also about this resentment. He said:

It is felt that whereas the dictum 'consider the individual child' is an admirable one, few training college lecturers consider the needs of the individual teacher when the question of method is discussed. Personality types can rarely be altered, not even by an intense course in Child Psychology, and most modern methods make great demands on the personality of the teacher. This question involves the whole business of teacher training and teacher selection; most teachers feel that it is unfair to have imposed upon them methods with which they cannot identify themselves.

I think you will agree with me that, as well as considered judgement and sincere feeling, this statement reveals a certain amount of anxiety and repudiation. The writer is saying: human nature cannot change—leave me as I am. But from his earlier remark we see how much he values co-operation and enquiry. I believe this expresses the views of a large number of teachers and their unsettled attitude towards their own need for help. What teachers mean, in part at least, when they resent the imposition of methods with which they cannot identify themselves is that they are afraid of the space between what they have made their own and what they have not. We may feel that we have to bridge this gap for them by providing tips and techniques, giving timely advice, and so on. Such things are of course helpful, though perhaps not always in the way we imagine. What matters is often the helpfulness more than the particular help we give. I hope you will not misunderstand me here. I am not trying to suggest that method has no significance in itself. I think those of us responsible for guiding teachers need to be both as imaginative and as logical about method as possible—to make a wealth of suggestions, pointing particularly to those we have found useful or seen other people use to advantage; more than this, to analyse methods in terms of children's interests. But this is by no means the whole of the guiding process, especially when we are dealing with the people who find experiment difficult; these are very often the people who fight shy of modern methods, though many of them are, almost secretly, strongly drawn towards them. If we are imaginative people we know intuitively that danger is the way to safety; but this by no means ensures the courage to face strange situations.

Obviously it is not the main function of inspectors to shield and guard teachers. Their first responsibility is to the children. What then are we to do in the face of this fear of change, this stubborn resolve to identify oneself with only a part of oneself and deny children the whole richness of a personality which is needed to nourish and strengthen their own?

I think the question has a good deal to do with the very human problem of the rights of possession. The teacher is in a sense asking: Whose children are they? Whose imagination is it? He may be feeling that if he leaves the mark of his influence upon them he has robbed them of something of their own. The same question may be asked of the person who comes into the lesson. Are you, by imposing something on me that I feel does not belong to me, doing to me what I fear I may be doing to the children? Or he may argue another way round. Some teachers are angry when they have to receive suggestions and ideas which were already their own as if they were not. I suffered like this as a child. I used to say to my mother, 'Don't always tell me what I am just going to do.' I think it was because this early experience was such a strong part of my sympathy, as well of my fear, that I was able to understand what was happening the other day in a student's teaching practice. I would like to describe this in some detail because it shows that my own identification was both a help and a hindrance.

The student was in many ways gifted, though he had not won high honours academically. He entered upon his teaching practice with a trepidation he did not try to conceal. In the first term he had been a member of a class to which I was lecturing on original composition in the English lesson. I read a large number of children's poems and the group was, I could see, excited and interested but also sceptical and on the defensive. They had the attitude of the man who looked at the giraffe in the zoo and said: 'I don't believe there *is* such an animal.' However, this student embarked on the method very early on in his practice in a Secondary Modern School. The children soon began to reward his trust in them with delightful compositions. He was staggered by the results. He copied out phrases and lines from their work and dwelt upon them lovingly, almost dotingly, and slowly became very possessive of them. Then he began to see the differences between one child and another, the variety of ideas which one child would express, and his excitement grew. He was richer than he knew. His confidence developed in other ways, relationships with the staff became very friendly; discipline problems which were marked at first became negligible. However, his attitude towards me underwent a change. He was aware that with the children and staff he could hold his ground as a creator and producer—with me I think he felt he had stolen something, but also, and as his confidence grew, that I was taking something from him.

When I had first suggested a lesson in verse composition, he had said he was afraid to begin. However when I offered on this occasion to take the first lesson for him, his face darkened and he said, 'I want to do it on my own, my own way, but I would like you to be there.' The lesson was arranged and I witnessed a fine tight-rope performance. He told me afterwards how frightened he had been and I was able to reply with truth, 'You didn't show it, you did it beautifully.' To which he replied, 'I don't mind telling you now that when you read those poems to us last term no one really believed that children had written them.' He could not confess this until he was established himself in the method.

However, it was not as simple as that. The work went on and I did not see him again that term. Later, I had a letter, full of the same ecstatic pleasure and surprise, giving me two poems in full. After the first he wrote, 'in case you should think this is an isolated example, here is another'; and at the end he remarked, 'Will they ever believe me when I tell them about this next term?' In my reply I pointed out that these imaginative powers are in most children and he had the gift of believing in them; but it took a little time for him to be able to forgive me for being the one who first suggested the idea to him. Then in a further letter he pointed out how the work was progressing: 'just as you said'— and he thanked me for the encouragement he was given to go forward with his ideas. We had become equals not only in fact but also in recognition and acknowledgement.

One can see what a hair's breadth there is for some people between success and failure, and how a method which a teacher can feel himself at one with can both stabilize his own personality and at the same time liberate creative powers in children. It is also important to notice that I was able to be a real help only when I became aware of my own identification—but he was largely responsible for showing it to me. At one point I was about to build bridges—in fact to take over the whole construction—but he showed his resentment at just the right point and the creativeness of both of us was saved. In other cases I have found that students were anxious for me to take the lesson and that was the only way to give them confidence. Sometimes I have shared lessons with them: but I was wrong in imagining that either of these methods was appropriate for this teacher. A great deal depends upon the fundamental attitude in the personality towards possessing and being possessed—'influencing and being influenced.'[1]

It is relevant here to mention one of the discoveries I made during a piece of research into the writing of original composition.[2] It was found with children that, when they first began to write, many of them imitated poems from anthologies or borrowed lines and phrases here and there. If these efforts were accepted in the degree to which they were original, and not condemned in the parts that were not, that is providing one was able to make such a clear distinction, the writers soon began to use their own idioms and rhythms; though of course unconscious imitation is one of the ways in which we reflect upon our origins. But so disturbing do many teachers find the 'stealing' stage that they fight shy of the work altogether. So we find the Promethean struggle recurring in these classroom dramas which can indeed in some people take on titanic proportions in the mind.

[1] See the article of D. W. Winnicott, 'On influencing and being influenced' in *The Child, the family and the Outside World*, Penguin Books, 1964, pp. 199 ff.

[2] The research was carried out at the Institute of Education, The University of Leeds 1951–1953, and part of it has been published in *Coming into their Own*, Marjorie Hourd and Gertrude Cooper. Heinemann, 1959.

One of the difficulties in guiding people whom we cannot see very often is that of becoming aware of what is going on—of being able to place it in a total situation: and this means trying to understand the teacher almost in a philosophical sense. The other day I heard of a case of an Art teacher whose work was being examined in an inspection and the inspector felt that the teacher was not encouraging children to look at things enough and she made an excellent suggestion, though, I gathered, with an over-enthusiasm. She suggested: 'send the children into the garden to bring in all the brown things they can find; and then let them pick delphiniums and forget-me-nots and look at them until they really know what brownness and blueness is.' Now it happened that this teacher was in a stage of transition in her own development as an artist. She had at one time perhaps overstressed the assertions of the outside world, and she was now giving more place to the symbol. No doubt this was reflected in her teaching. The inspector may have been on a wave of reaction against what might have seemed to her over-emphasis on fantasy. Obviously we are placed here at the heart of a problem which has beset philosophers from Plato onwards, if not before. We find two people moving in opposite directions in their need to solve it, but little attempt was made to try and understand what was happening and to share a mystery. The teacher was not as able to express the necessary arrogance and still enlist the inspector's co-operation as my student was. However, she was fortunate in having a Head who knew her work in a total picture and supported her in the teeth of a bad report. Not many teachers could easily survive the life and death struggle of the student, or the rejection given to the teacher unless someone was there to lend support and sanction; however, I have known many teachers saved by inspectors who valued their work even though they were pioneering alone and unsupported in a school.

We are really dealing with the psychology of change and transition; and the fear of dispossession and loss of continuity which gives rise to a need for definition. We hear a good deal these days about the rarity of finding teachers who base their work on a fundamental philosophy; and yet most teachers have philosophic minds. How then has this situation occurred? Is it not true that most of us go through 'philosophic'[1] stages, particularly in the teens and early twenties, schools of thought and ideologies of various kinds gain a hold and then gradually life itself soaks them up—maxims, platitudes and great thoughts are bargained with, bought back or discarded; a stream of philosophic enquiry accompanies the daily life of most thinking people but so little of it is ever thought through to the point of formulation. It is not taken into the mind in a way which can prompt action and change custom. It is as though we were living in a philosophic age without a working philosophy. One of the difficulties is that we can no longer leave philosophy to the philosophers alone; too much has happened and we are gaining knowledge through the social sciences which is stated in such a way that all of us are involved in the here-and-now implications of it. It is of course psychology in particular which assails the teacher in this way. Again let us listen to the man we first quoted, who does in so many ways seem to represent the average teacher. Under the heading of psychology he writes:

> Perhaps the greatest impact upon the school scene in recent years has been made by the psychologist. It is true that teachers are not fully adjusted to the situation. It is not difficult to find the reason why. A teacher's training course, at the most occupying three years, cannot completely cover the huge field of child psychology. Moreover it is in itself a dynamic subject, requiring constant up-to-date reading and revision of subjective opinion. Teachers are apt to snap at the end products of psychological research and to employ methods in practice of which they themselves are not convinced. Teachers working without conviction are a menace to the profession.

Now the interesting point about this statement is that it fails to take into account the fact that modern dynamic psychology is built upon the implicit assumption that the child is father to

---

[1] Using the term in a general, attributive sense.

the man, and that a teacher needs to keep up not only his reading but his living in such a way that the child and the man in himself are brought together in harmony. The problem for us in this modern age is not how to escape conflict but how to be at home within it; and as soon as we try to do that, then we discover how far there is a basis of sound principle. The war between activity and formal methods of teaching has always been waged inside our own minds. We cannot solve it by placing it outside as a matter only for pedagogic debate. The students did not accept the validity of the children's poems, because they could not believe that they were written without preparatory lessons in prosody—could not in fact believe that the poetic spirit is part of our human heritage and, as soon as we gain a vocabulary, part of our human culture. Further, part of our moral stature. For when we face an empty canvas it is our love that is on trial as Robert Graves understood in the *White Goddess*, when he wrote (quoting from Alun Lewis): 'The single poetic theme is of Life and Death—the question of what survives of the beloved.'[1]

To sum up very briefly, my plea is that we should try to maintain a kind of two-way influence of knowledge upon minds, and minds upon knowledge, and recognize the defining function which method takes within this process. A teacher is unlikely to bring a child to the point of clarity when he can say 'I've got it'—'I see it'—'I understand' unless he has been able in his own mind to make the facts he is presenting his own. The child will then feel he is understanding both a truth about things and a truth about the imagination which presents them; for this is how he first came to recognize the world in the person of his mother both as a fact of perception and as the fulfilment of what in his intense need and desire he imagined. A loving mother can so shape the growing child's imagination that learning will be to him both the satisfaction of curiosity and the possibility of new vision. It would seem then that the greatest service we can render a teacher is to establish his confidence in what is his own.

[1] See Hourd and Cooper, *Coming into their Own*, Heinemann, 1959, p. 23.

## CHAPTER NINE

# Guidance in Training Teachers[1]

This is an attempt in a short space to look at some aspects of 'guidance' in the special setting of teacher training. It is not intended as a criticism of prevailing methods, but rather as an examination of some of the guiding processes within teacher training. Following this aim, no naming references are made to particular ventures, nor are requirements peculiar to different institutions considered in detail nor in comparison. Much of significance is doubtless left out, the area is too wide for justice to be done to every facet of what is one of the most fruitful experimental fields in education.

### The Backbone of the Curriculum

Most people are aware of the shape which the main part of the curriculum takes in the majority of training institutions in England. Lectures are given, essays and examination papers set and corrected, theses and seminars tutored, and lessons prepared, listened to, criticized and assessed. Differences of emphasis occur. For example, a few colleges omit examinations and many in addition place a high value upon heuristic methods through which the student pursues on his own a personal interest as a minor investigation or engages in a group study. Methodology, principles of education, history of education, psychology and child study have become the backbone of the training college curriculum, along with individual or group projects and, of course, teaching practice. On the whole this general scheme

[1] This article is republished from *The Yearbook of Education;* 1955, pp. 302–309.

suits the students' needs to a large extent. But tutors also have in mind that maturity is the greatest asset a teacher can have, and so aim at turning out people who can think and act for themselves. Individual differences in tutors and students both help and hinder such growth in independence, and few would doubt that it is a common bond of interest in the same subject or group of ideas which contributes most at this point. This closer contact of minds is facilitated by a tutorial system shaped to particular requirements. In these groups of a few people, likenesses and differences can be appreciated at a time when help is at hand. However, as intimate feelings and ideas under these conditions are likely to be disclosed, a courtesy is needed which leaves room for both spontaneity and reticence.

### The Effects of Different Groupings on the Quality of Guidance

It is found in practice that the more various the groupings, the more chance there is for mental manoeuvre of a kind likely to result in thinking for oneself. The large lecture or assembly, where a community sense can be experienced, and yet where anonymity assists long-term digestion, is one pattern: the topic discussion group of about fifteen to thirty people is another, in which individual response is more easily recognizable and the tutor cannot remain unaware of those he has inspired or bored, or left high and dry. And so on. Voluntary or compulsory attendance also alters the quality of the 'guidance' at work. Where the voluntary principle is a guiding factor tutors will have to school themselves to bear with what could be called 'depression caused by diminution' and equally, of course, 'elation caused by unexpected increase'. Students too will be called upon to review their consciences. However, it is not always wise to refrain from bringing some pressure to bear upon obtaining for others what we know to be good. Gratitude for this is often expressed by students.

Again, the quality of 'guidance' in groups is also affected by considerations of time and space, especially the former. Courses of one year are bound to bring in guiding factors different from those involved in a two- or three-year course. Very complex psychological issues arise here, which cannot be entered upon within the scope of this essay. We have to look at time and place factors. For example people are more prepared to deepen understanding if they are sure they will not be interrupted at vulnerable or crucial points. Place also holds some significance, and particularly seating arrangements. It has been found, for instance, that the circular group responds differently from the straight-row group, the degree of personal commitment being greater in the former. This is a cursory glance only at a cluster of influences which never remains static and which contains, as well as what can be planned for and predicted, a large number of incalculable factors arising partly from society outside the college and from unconscious forces within the personality. 'Guidance', to be effective, has to allow for what is not known as well as for what is evident.

*Directive Guidance*

On the whole, the methods described above call for a directive form of 'guidance' on the basis of a tutor-student relationship of the teacher-pupil prototype. Within the orbit of this directive 'guidance' the student finds himself linked to a tradition which lends a feeling of continuity and enhances his prestige within a new profession. Slowly he comes to realize that the future lies with him, which gives scope to his reconstructive urges. All this would be true, too, of schools and universities, but for training courses it holds as nowhere else. After a few weeks, or months of the course, the student in training realizes that he is learning in a new way. A young graduate remarked at this point: 'I am tired of thinking for myself.' The tutor asked whether she did not think for herself during the university course, and the reply was 'Yes, but not to such an extent in terms of myself.'

This discovery is put to the test during the first teaching practice. To be in front of a class for the first time is an experience which calls up very strong feelings. The student is now not only aware that he is thinking in terms of himself, but that soon he will know in this new situation what terms he is on with himself. The teacher-pupil relationship is in reverse; the pupil has taken over the role of authority: it is because all this has happened before in his wishes and imagination that the event is both strange and familiar. He played at schools as a child, took opportunities to teach his fellows and his teachers when at school—even imagined himself in the place of his parents. But such daring was protected. He could, for example, pack up his fantasy play and go home to lunch, where his mother and father mercifully directed operations. Now a situation has taken place where there is no turning back. It is not enough to argue that now he is grown up, because it is common experience that this is a gradual process, and does not happen overnight. So we must allow the student to know that it takes a long time to make a good teacher. Further, he needs 'guidance' at this juncture of a kind which he has not required in quite the same way hitherto. Head teachers and assistant staff are now added to his group of counsellors, and they also want to understand how they can best guide students training in their schools through this difficult stage. The remark is often heard that a teacher either has got the ability to hold a class or he has not, and nothing can be done about it. But we know from the work in classes of teachers which is taking place with appreciable success under the auspices of institutes of education that much more can be discovered after years of experience about the dynamics of teaching. The question is: How far can we assume that human nature is capable of change?

## Contributions from the Social Sciences

This enquiry is not, of course, limited to spheres of education. In fact it might be said that the problem of change is the most urgent for the world to-day. Two factors are chiefly responsible for this. One is the threat from outside in the shape of the hydrogen bomb and totalitarian ideologies.[1] and the other is the fact that the social sciences are making much more known about

[1] Note the date of this article—1955!

the moving forces within man and society. Need and knowledge to some extent go hand in hand. It is easier to express the one when the other is in sight. Yet scientific knowledge is often won by those who are prepared to ask questions to which no answer is foreseeable. At all events, some training colleges are recognizing the relevance of these newer branches of learning; in particular sociology; anthropology, and dynamic psychology— and they are not only adding lectures and seminars upon them but are making a search within these disciplines for techniques which might make 'guidance' less dependent upon instruction and intuition and more directly governed by a knowledge of the dynamics of change.

Social scientists have chosen the small group of from seven to ten people as an instrument in these researches. The literature dealing with group dynamics has reached formidable proportions. Here we shall look at ways in which some teacher training institutions are taking up this work. Various discussion methods are used—from those in which a topic is followed in a formalized way, at one extreme, to those in which therapeutic techniques are employed, at the other. So far, however, the adoption of interpretative groups on psycho-analytic lines has not gone far in teacher training in England;[1] but with the increase in the number of educationists who have been analysed this state of affairs will alter. It is important to give these groups careful scrutiny at all levels. One of the difficulties is that participation in them, particularly the analytic ones, is essential to full understanding—a fact which often causes mistrust. This, however, should not be put instead of scholarly caution. On the whole the leader of the small group—analysed or not, as the case may be—is a person who has a flair for inducing others to express ideas and problems freely in such a way that greater awareness occurs, followed by a change of attitude. Authority is not abnegated, but, through 'guidance', placed where it can be studied.

[1] Since 1955 more studies of Group-work of this kind have appeared. See for example Elizabeth Richardson, *Group Study for Teachers*, Routledge & Kegan Paul, The Student's Library of Education.

## Group Dynamics

This shift of focus reflects what happened to the student who knew she was thinking in terms of herself. At this point of change students frequently express their anxiety by becoming very critical of tutors, whilst at the same time making stronger demands upon their help and resources. The imaginative tutor recognizes these growing-points and, if he can associate himself with the change that is occurring, he may be able to extend the student's vision, and frequently his own. In the group similar things happen. Through the give-and-take among a small number of people members are able to examine more minutely than they can alone the complexity of the impulses activating their ideas; the workings, for example, of prejudice and reason in argument, of conversion and conviction as qualities of thought. They come to recognize in themselves the co-existence of opposite feelings, particularly of friendliness and hostility towards the same person. They are, as a result, more willing to accept tension as a normal factor in productivity.

In sensitive people these discoveries are not made, nor change suffered, without a certain amount of depression. This, too, they are more able to accept and even acknowledge as an enrichment. It is impossible to take part in this work, either as a leader or as member, without becoming vividly aware of the existence within oneself of a society—which is closely bound up with that within the group—and of how far this reflects society outside. Such insight influences teaching method, as one member put it, 'at the roots'. It will have become evident that the people most benefited by those revelations are those with a fair degree of stability, whose interest and curiosity drive them to self-enquiry and social investigation. The importance of making membership voluntary cannot be overstressed. Even so, it is possible that people will enlist in groups who would be better served by individual psycho-therapy, or by some quite different means of 'guidance'. They can, of course be so advised, though it is not always possible to know who they are at the outset, just as there is no infallible prognostic instrument for selection of candidates for teacher training. Whatever view is taken of making these discussion groups a part of the training course, their research value should not be overlooked.

## Creative Groups

One of the most fruitful lines of research for the future, in the view of the writer, is the investigation of how far and in what ways the findings of modern dynamic psychology can help, at the teacher source, methods in the classroom to be revitalized. To put this another way, we need to know more of how imagination works in terms of self and other people at one and the same time. There are signs that these more subtle forms of 'guidance' are being sought through the many creative groups appearing, among both tutors and students, in training colleges and departments of education; groups in painting, pottery (especially modelling), music and movement, spontaneous mime and drama and poetry writing, where the accent is not on the acquiring of techniques and standards—though these factors enter of themselves—but upon direct expression of thought and feeling in a self-chosen medium. The discussion group can belong to this category if words are used as a creative medium. One member of a discussion-writing group remarked: 'I found that the experience of wrestling with words (for I am not a verbalist) seemed to put the problems concerning human beings in relation to each other in their right proportions.' The art groups reveal as well, how, as individuality is gained and recognized through a medium, social unity is strengthened, and yet at the same time how the group helps to release the individual's thoughts and expression. Many also find that the recognition of the self in a composition takes place at much the same time as mastery over the material. The work bristles with points of discovery; but it needs time, opportunities and 'educated perceptions' if its significance is to be understood in terms of psychology and art together, and applied to classroom procedures.

It is not easy to describe or even detect the many forms of

'guidance' which may enter this work, yet they undoubtedly relate to experience outside the arts. Moreover, many of them are implicit in the more instructional, directed, or therapeutic methods, which succeed mainly on the waves of inspiration, or through the skilful application of 'the third ear' which catches the unconscious vibrations of the mind. Special qualities are needed in 'guidance' of this kind, aptly defined in Keats' phrase 'negative capability': that expectant attitude in which the tutor is prepared to accept whatever comes, to take on what Keats in another place, describes as 'the chameleon nature of the poet'.

## Negative and Positive Factors

It would seem that on the whole this 'negative' form of guidance has not received its rightful place in education, and for a reason it is not far to seek. The teacher is afraid that in accepting every form of expression he might countenance what is bad, and so lower standards. But 'countenancing', to coin a word for the present argument, includes acknowledgement and judgement. For a person not only wants to have his ideas accepted in the mind of someone else; he wants to know what happens to them there. It is common experience that advice can be taken and weighed most readily from a person who has accepted one, as we say, 'for one's own sake'. Those who have had a good deal of experience in watching students teach, and have tried to describe the performance to them afterwards with approbation and criticism mingled, will have noticed what a remarkable effect this has on the next perfomance. They feel they belong somewhere. They have been put into a picture, yet their mobility and capacity for change are recognized. Again, this use of framework and flexibility together is essential within the design of a training course if countenancing in its two aspects is to reap rewards.

This countenancing of the person as one would a work of art involves taking all qualities together in the appreciation of the design before judgement is passed. As Keats writes of the poetical character: 'It has no character—it enjoys light and shade; it lives in gusto, be it foul or fair, high or low, rich or poor mean or elevated. It has as much delight in conceiving an Iago as an Imogen. What shocks the virtuous philosopher delights the chameleon poet. It does no harm from its relish of the dark side of things any more than from its taste for the bright one; because they both end in speculation.'[1] We know, however, from his life how susceptible Keats was to praise and blame, and how much the standard of his work meant to him.

## Psychology, Art and Education

These reflections present only a few examples of how dynamic psychology and art criticism come together to elucidate matters of first concern to educationists also. An imaginative person works along these lines intuitively; others can be helped by knowing a little more of what it is all about. Discoverers benefit from a map—even though every point has not yet been charted. It is, however, not meant to suggest that these forms of 'guidance' bring about changes, far-reaching though they may be, of the radical kind affected by psycho-analysis. We are concerned here with change that is within the scope of the educationist—and how psycho-analytical discoveries as well as poetry and art can support and illuminate. For the teacher is closely concerned most of the time with human nature in all its complexity. A student, for example, who does not feel accepted as a whole person, and whose fundamental security was perhaps threatened in early times, will be likely, if challenged too far in respect of discipline or in the use of activity methods, to react either by repudiating the standards involved in these things or by underestimating himself. These responses can often be modified if he meets with someone who can accept his dark and light side together—and do this with gusto. For Keats in this phrase has hit upon a quality of 'guidance' which more perhaps than any other inspires and strengthens—the quality in a teacher of enthusiasm and delighted enjoyment of the world. The student's own appetite is thus sanctioned, and his eyes, as a result, opened to wider horizons.

[1] From a letter to R. Woodhouse, October 1818.

*In Conclusion*

We have seen, then, how, in the field of teacher training, there has been a continuous effort to satisfy the student's need for 'guidance', to keep in touch with new developments of thought, and to preserve the best in past experience. A mid-way territory such as this is an easy target for attack. But certainly there is now a tendency to regard 'guidance' towards maturity as more important than instruction and advice; and to recognize the extent and nature of the difficulties which lie in the way of such striving. It is suggested here that one form of guidance holds a crucial position because it influences stability at the roots. Its aim is to ensure continuity within change, structure within originality; for which a quality of understanding is required that is partial and discriminating at the same time as it is catholic and chameleon.

Are we asking too much of 'the teacher of teachers'—the integrity of the scholar, scientist, healer and artist? This, anyhow, is what he asks of himself, but with the emphasis upon the character nearest his own genius. Nothing is more detrimental to guiding forces than methods imposed from without in an arbitrary fashion. Room should be made for the tried and tested to remain, along with fresh ideas to be carried out where they are acceptable. For 'guidance' to be effective should bring need and knowledge together in such a way as to leave room for what has yet to be imagined.

# PART THREE

# Continuity and Reciprocity

This is the cardinal characteristic which distinguishes human thought from animal response—the ability to distinguish A from B while at the same time recognizing that A and B are somehow interdependent.

from *Lévi-Strauss* by Edmund Leach

# CHAPTER TEN

# English and Continuity[1]

## 1. Introduction

As soon as one is unable any more to take a thing for granted then it becomes a subject of special concern. This is what has happened to continuity and the sense of continuity. According to the dictionary the law of continuity states that all changes in nature are continuous and not abrupt. On the strength of this law we naturally look for gradual change within the environment. Today however change on all sides has become so abrupt, so massive and so rapid that we are not able to account for it altogether within our expectations and we are left with the problem of how to adapt to society without losing contact with ourselves. Children and young people need help in dealing with this issue of continuity within change, however awkwardly they may at times reach out for it.

Richard Hoggart put his finger on it recently when he said that students today are talking from within themselves and that they are trying to understand who and what they are as human beings. This is where we so often fail them educationally. Understandably perhaps we are so concerned with the content of our subject and the methods adopted 'to put it across' as we say that we are inclined to forget those processes at work that relate to being human, yet now we need their help more than ever. In education the word 'discipline' is often employed by people who

---

[1] The following article is the text of the opening lecture delivered to the annual conference of the National Association of Teachers of English at Exeter University, April 1970 and published later in *English in Education*, vol 4, No 2, pp. 14–25 in association with Oxford University Press.

see the pupil or student as a person held to order whilst highly controlled knowledge is imparted to him. If however the pupil is regarded as a person as well, with resources of his own, the whole view of his status as a learner changes—his own abilities become intrinsic to the knowledge being absorbed. This is not an easy idea to grasp and there are many ways of stating it as we shall discover. However, at any level and within any subject within the curriculum it is wasteful to neglect what Wordsworth called 'the powers that work for us'. To put it very briefly this lecture is about some of the powers that work for us within the literature lesson and the relationships between them.

## 2. *Finding out about Growing up*

I have tried in this paper to suggest, and develop so far, the notion of reciprocal process in education with the help of some ideas moving through contemporary thought. Fundamental to those ideas is the concern for people as human beings, a concern which is obviously behind the strong interest taken today in growing up—an interest which children share. They listen for the authentic note of their own striving as it is struck here for example in these lines from a young girl's poem.

> The growing mind is a growing thirst—
> That so teased with a stale wisdom
> Searches for water, ice-slipping, light-distilled;
> Craves for the articulation of its own truth.

I have often thought, mischievously no doubt, that children are the only people who believe in education. A problem for us now is that they are beginning to think so too!

At all events growing up is news today. Through the mass media we are treated hour by hour to the latest information on the life span. The well-known American psychologist, Erik Erikson has envisaged this span as falling into eight stages—not appearing in strict chronology but as inter-acting, overlapping and synchronizing. One period he makes out is contained in another and yet remains distinct. We are several ages at the same time yet one predominates. Wordsworth said that he brought back 'remotest infancy' through the vigour of his thoughts; today we are not so dependent on the strength of recall, and periods of development are studied through their influence on each other and in great detail through experimental and clinical observations which take us back via babyhood to birth and parturition, thence to the womb, which often catches the headlines these days—and forward via adolescence to maturity and old age. Thus development moves backwards and forwards yet continuity is of its essence if all goes well. I do not know how any teacher today can do without a knowledge of development.

### 3. *Psychology and Literature*
The teacher of English however has never been able to escape these questions even if he wanted to because of the long association between psychology and literature and because language is an intrinsic part of growing up. Language ensures continuity especially through speech and sound, which are ineradicably linked to our first perceptions. In fact the baby's babblings are significant in the growth of language as a whole.

As psychological knowledge has penetrated more deeply the fabric of society so it has become more explicit in literature as we are seeing for example in so much modern literature. The works of Saul Bellow and Samuel Beckett provide good examples. In very different ways they chime in with current speculation about the significance for development of early body feelings. Beckett's recent sound play entitled *Breath*, is attracting serious attention as well of course as a certain amount of idle curiosity. It seems to me that in as far as this thirty-seconds play is an enactment of the birth cry it is in logical progression from *Waiting for Godot* which depicts, as I have always seen it, on one level, the waste-lands and expectations of parturition. When some years ago Professor M. M. Lewis suggested that there was a link between the cry of rage at birth and the howlings of King Lear few people at that time realized what a profound and significant statement he had made about continuity. Again it must be remarked children are cottoning on to these explorations in medicine, psychology and literature by connecting them up with their own interest in the body as a source of ideas.

## 4. *Literature and ourselves*

What all this means is that much of literature today is providing a medium through which the reader can establish himself in his own eyes *at the same time as* he enters the lives of others in books. The understanding between writer and reader on this basis is mutually nourishing, and it should render unnecessary those rather tiresome discussions about whether literature should be studied in its own right or whether it should be thrown over to interpretation through personal experience. Nothing detracts more from the serious enjoyment of a novel for instance than the frequent intrusion of one's own or other people's associations. On the other hand nothing is more empty than a book in which you cannot find yourself. The literature and life controversy has to be resolved within the exchanges of literature itself. But here children often need the teacher's mediation. They can gain most from a book if at first they hear it, or parts of it, read aloud. As I believe the reading-aloud lesson to be a focal point in our work in English, I would like to say a little more about it; but first let us obtain a picture of the network of relationships at the centre of which the teacher places himself in the good reading lesson.

## 5. *Reciprocity in the Reading Lesson*

There are several partners and groups sharing in the literary experience in the classroom. There is the child with the book, the teacher with the book, the child, the book and other children —the teacher, the child and the book as well as, what is often forgotten, the book and the author. A writer is an audience to himself. 'I attend to the unfolding of my thought' writes Arthur Rimbaud, 'I watch and listen.' Then there is the question of the manifest and latent meanings in a piece of writing. 'The author may have thought he was not dealing with himself,' says

Ionesco 'yet he discovers himself in his work.' Finally there is the child who as a writer himself finds his stimulus in the writings of others.

The way in which the teacher gathers together all these threads in the reading lesson is the essence and proof of his teaching skill, and whilst it is going on he must try not to get into the position of the centipede which, when it realized that it had a hundred legs, became paralysed with fright. He must keep his eye on the ball, on the experiencing of a passage within his own mind, remembering that his best work comes from teaching *with* his knowledge—not from teaching *it*. It is the strength and integrity of his own attitude to literature that counts.

When he has chosen appropriate material, he begins to read to the class with that strange blend of closeness and apartness that marks his intentness. Slowly as a reader-writer relationship unfolds in his awareness so it begins to come about in the pupil's. It is a mutually differentiating process in which two people lay claim to their own functioning. The teacher during this performance is a person in his own right who is delegating power whilst he is in possession of it and the pupil becomes a person in his own right because he is taking the work of literature into his own identification system, a work as we have seen already prepared through its own inner relationships for this incorporation. We must remember that the sense of identity is closely linked with the sense of continuity.

Experience shows that these exchanges in the reading lesson hang upon delicate threads. I have noted repeatedly that when reading aloud if a firm contact is lost for a time with the material, an arbitrary note creeps in, ideas are joined together, fusion is interrupted and the attention of the class begins to flag. After reading to students I have sometimes asked them whether they could point out when a loss of interest began to take place and invariably they point to just those places where I noted my own lessening of grip upon the argument or story. Once children however are aware of the teacher's confidence in his material they begin to ask questions that are both relevant to the passage and to their own understanding of it. It is quite unnecessary, especially at first, for the teacher to begin to ask questions. Instead, as soon as the passage has been read and a decent pause allowed for, he should require various children to read it back. Once they have experienced their own response growing more distinct as the teacher reads, it is surprising how well they will read to the class afterwards, and even backward or retarded children, if enough basic trust has been established, will take heart, and show us that assimilation has begun. If however we lose faith in our capacity to give a passage a life of its own we are likely to fall back on one gimmick or another, splitting off parts for dissection and examination before they have been grasped as functions of the whole, then

> How with this rage shall beauty hold a plea,
> Whose action is no stronger than a flower?

## 6. *The Strength of Aesthetic Experience*

So we must take courage and not feel guilty when all we seem to do in a lesson is to read well and give children the chance to do the same. Good reading lessons have been going on for a long time and teachers have probably never fully realized what strength they have brought—a strength of vision comparable to that which arises when we look at a work of art and when as Adrian Stokes has phrased it, we 'enjoy relationships with delineated processes that enliven our own'. In his inspiring essay *The Invitation in Art*, he uses terms very close to those I have just been employing, as when speaking of poetry he writes: 'A poem, like a picture, properly appreciated stands away from us as an object on its own, but the poetry that has gripped, the poetry of which it is composed, when read as an unfolding process, combines with corresponding processes in a reader who lends himself.'[1]

A new psychology of aesthetics is emerging which should help students in training to deal with aesthetic responses in those whom they contact in schools and with a confidence gained from

---

[1] p. 19.

an experience of their own. These responses are of course not limited to literature or pictorial art, they apply to sculpture, architecture and music as Stokes brilliantly illustrates in his books. They also apply to film and television. Eisenstein in his book *The Film Sense* points out how the spectator can be drawn into a creative act without his individuality being subordinated to the author's—rather he says 'it is opened up throughout the process of fusion with the author's intention'. He quotes Marx's definition of the course of genuine investigation which echoes the argument here: 'Not only the result, but the road to it, also is part of the truth. The investigation of truth must itself be true; true investigation is unfolded truth.'[1] (It is interesting the way this word 'unfolded' keeps cropping up.) It strikes me that it is probably because teachers of English have been dealing with 'unfolded truth' for many generations that they have not fallen quite as easily as some colleagues have into the controversy about traditional and discovery methods of teaching. In a true unfolding, what has been and what is about to be make one entity.

## 7. Self-expression and Communication

It is obvious in the light of all I have been saying so far that communication cannot be thought of as what E. H. Gombrich, another distinguished contemporary art critic, calls 'a simple parcel-post method of exchange'. 'A person,' he writes, 'thinks all he need do is to transform his emotion into an expressive configuration and send it across to a sensitive beholder who will unwrap the parcel and take out the emotion.'[2] Such a view reminds one of the old slogan 'no impression without expression' —an injunction still followed in arbitrary fashion in many classrooms. The child in these lessons often finds himself in a vacuum—and teachers may wonder when they take in the odd verses and illustrations, watch the so-called spontaneous dramas, where it all leads. I am referring of course only to expression in which the child has no real stake and where inner relationship is lacking—'Self expression and art are not synonymous,' declares

[1] p. 35.     [2] *Meditations on a Hobby Horse*, p. 54.

Adrian Stokes, and one should add neither are self-expression and the having of a self to express. I have no doubt in my own mind that everything a child writes is significant if we know how to de-code it in development terms—but it does not mean that everything is of equal significance in aesthetic terms. Eventually the two must merge. This merging I have dealt with over the years in some detail. What I have tried to suggest here is that the ability to establish reciprocal relationship is essential for the appreciation of literature—but as well it is essential for the maintenance of a sense of continuity. If communication is no longer to be thought of as a matter of crude exchange—then continuity is no longer to be considered as a simple description of successive events. Time is an aspect of the self.

## 8. *Continuity and the Chronological System*

There is no doubt that we have been held back from obtaining a full vision of man's creative powers by the injunction for so long laid upon culture to represent continuity chronologically. I recently came upon a pamphlet of the English Association containing the Presidential address of 1922 by Edmund Gosse, entitled 'The Continuity of Literature,' in the course of which he declared: 'I shall defend with my last breath the chronological system.' It was only such a system, he maintained, that could discover the deep unity of purpose through all the manifestations of literature, He was looking for the generalizing function of literature mainly within content, and by means of comparative study as we are still doing in our setting of examination papers. Had he looked for it as well in terms of shared process, in the way we have been trying to do, he would have been bound to come in touch with the challenge to the chronological system being made under his very nose. As Lévi-Strauss has pointed out it is not to be thought that history has no meaning but that we need to take in other ways of looking at things in order to include other dimensions.[1]

[1] A conversation with Claude Lévi-Strauss, G. A. Steiner, *Encounter*, April 1966.

## 9. *Continuity in the Form of Simultaneity*

It so happened that I went to University in 1922, and I certainly was quite unaware, in my academic fastness and in those days before mass media, of the dramatic changes taking place in the wider culture of the time. This revolution was summed up by Virginia Woolf when she declared: 'In 1910 human nature changed.' The critic Walter Allen spells out some of the cultural events referred to in that remark[1]—1910 was the year of the exhibition in London of the post-impressionists in which Van Gogh, Gauguin, Cézanne and Picasso among others were shown to the British public for the first time. He mentions other events, the most influential of which he supposes was the publication of *The Interpretation of Dreams* in 1900, though the book was not made available in this country in translation until 1913. What Freud virtually did in that book was to uncover a universal capacity, shown intitially in dreams, to dispense with chronological time and in his own words 'to discover logical connexion in the form of simultaneity'. He soon realized that the artist, if prepared to abandon representational modes, could greatly extend his grasp of the world through this way of thinking. It is of course the young child's way before he finds himself at the mercy of the chronological imperative. With infinite freshness the child is able to bring things together in his pictures from different places and times as though they were a community of the moment.

Most primary school teachers welcome the influence of these relational modes of expression found also in children's writings today as a relief from the interminable narratives that have in the past filled pages and pages of composition books—narratives in which the writer takes so long to get up in the morning and extricate himself from the family that he never reaches his objectives. Moreover he has to go through another palaver in order to get home again. Somewhere along the line the immediacy of the adventure he had set out to describe is lost. However, the forms of child expression are undergoing change in many respects and

[1] In *Tradition and Dream.*

as a result the gap between child and adult writing is appreciably lessening. It is very old-fashioned of the 'Black Papers' to be writing about child-centred education as though it were a thing of these times. What we have now is child-adult/adult-child education which is in the process of being defined.[1]

All these changes are turning armchair critics into field workers. The anthropologist tends more and more to involve himself in the life of the people he is studying, the linguist has left his text-book and the teacher his dais—some might say he has disappeared with it! Those distant figures conjured up by 'the Black Papers'—Froebel and Caldwell Cook for example— have long since been superceded. We are not looking now for missionary pioneers so much as for seminal thinkers and not looking for these bred only in education. The contemporary stage is filled with people converging from all sides upon education. There are creative writers, artists, sculptors, psychologists, psycho-analysts, film directors, critics, linguists, biologists, sociologists, anthropologists, ethologists—and so on. Who would have thought the age had made so many? These are the people students in training should be reading and arguing about passionately.

## 10. *The Either-or Mentality*

However, in following these guides we should all be careful to eschew what I call the either-or way of thinking which tries to avoid complexity by splitting off one set of ideas from another. We do not *have* to choose between learning by rote and learning by discovery—between authority and free discipline, correctness and free-expression, logical thought and imagination and so on. Children themselves are well aware of the inadequacy of this way of arguing. There is the story, familiar I expect to many of you, of the child in the progressive school who was growing rather tired of his label and when a visitor asked him what he was doing, he replied, 'lying about and developing'. One can see how

[1] See *Fight for Education* edited by C. B. Cox and A. E. Dyson (*Critical Quarterly*) and 'Crisis in Education', edited by C. B. Cox and Dyson (*Critical Quarterly*).

it is that children seek for themselves the in-between area of play where merging can safely take place. They look for a curriculum too in which the utmost flexibility can operate within a firm framework. They expect a school to be intaking as well as outgoing, as Marion Milner once put it. This is the area too where creative adults do their best work, an area where they can allow the free and the structured to meet, where they can summon up the courage to follow the free-play of ideas at the same time as they are bringing them under control. No one should imagine that this is easy.

The either-or distortion affects ideas prompting organization as well as methods of teaching in schools. It is a bad day for any establishment when administration and the exercise of imagination are placed on different shoulders. One person turns into a manipulator—and the other into an ineffectual angel. Difference understood as an indication of the true complexity of a situation can yield positive results—but when it is exploited to bolster up prejudice or support hierarchies, then it is bound to lead to destructive ends.

Again the field of psychological theory all too frequently turns into a battle ground. It should be enlarging to recognize that there are many roads to Rome—and that in the happy remark of Abraham Kaplan: 'Science begins to come of age only when it abandons the doctrine of immaculate perception.' And the solemn words of Freud come to mind as well: 'The complexity of human character dynamically moved in all directions very rarely accommodates itself to the arbitrament of a simple alternative, as our antiquated moral philosophy would have it.'[1]

All this must be taken to heart in the terms of this paper. It would not be helpful for example to set up yet another either-or in the shape of either chronological or simultaneous continuity, since both modes are enriching at different times in different situations. When we must rebel is when we are being forced into using methods inappropriate to the matter in hand—and rebel then with all our might.

[1] *The Interpretation of Dreams*—(1932 edition), p. 570.

## 11. *Learning what we already know*

It is so easy to get into a rut and just not to see the value of what lies around us. The trouble with so many of us is that we are better at supplying children with knowledge than we are at establishing in them what they already know—some of which is half hidden and some too familiar maybe for recognition. Dr Johnson referred to this paradox when he wrote: 'That which is obvious is not always known and that which is known is not always present.' Wordsworth whose language is so often the language of our times has described poetically the task of having to become what we already are. He speaks of the mind's *excursive* power and it strikes me that 'excursion' is a better word to describe a child's journeying with the intention to return than the rather pretentious word 'discovery', a precarious achievement at the best of times, which is left to the very few. The passage from Wordsworth occurs in *The Excursion* towards the end of Book IV:

> So build we up the Being that we are,
> Thus deeply drinking in the soul of things
> We shall be wise perforce; and while inspired
> By choice, and conscious that the will is free,
> Shall move unswerving, even as if impelled
> By strict necessity, along the path
> Of order and of good.

It is fascinating to observe how some modern linguists are furnishing us with a picture of the child's progress in language which re-inforces Wordsworth's statement about being wise perforce. They give us a child with a strong biological urge to absorb his language environment and as well one with a strong propensity for inventing rules and making his way amongst his own riches.

## 12. *Making Oneself Known to a Book*

This 'excursive power' mentioned by Wordsworth is undoubtedly today being employed adventurously in literature not only in composition but in what is expected of the reader. I have just been reading the novel by B. S. Johnson, *The Unfortunates*, which comes in a box containing twenty-seven sections held together by a removable wrapper. Apart from the first and last sections which are marked as such the other twenty-five are intended to be read in random order. I felt when reading this book, which I found very stimulating, that I was not so much making the book known to me in the way I had read books in the past as I was making myself known to the book—as when you explore many routes to the same destination you find you are learning about yourself as a traveller as much as you are familiarizing a district.

### 13. *Time and the Critic*

I realized as well how I had for a long time been groping for a principle in criticism that would account for those moments in reading a book or studying a passage when continuity appeared as a palpable presence—perhaps this has to do with the word being made flesh, a pronouncement one must go on trying to understand.

Marshall McLuhan in a recent statement suggested that we were living in post-history in the sense that through electronic discovery all the pasts that ever were are now present to our consciousness and that all the futures that will be are here now: 'We are post history and timeless.' I cannot understand this very far in electronic terms but I have always felt that the visionary power of a poem or a novel or a play is contained in every significant line within it. If literary criticism is to benefit from the dynamic approach which is prompting so much of the thinking within those other disciplines I have mentioned, we shall have to learn how to read excursively and how to experience a line or a passage in the moment of its unfolding. Let us take for example the well-known line from *Othello:*

Keep up your bright swords, for the dew will rust them.

Even as this is being spoken before the angry Brabantio and his retinue, the hurt enters Othello's mind as if between this line and the next he were crying out: 'Please don't do this to me.' Then he composes himself and his language:

> Good signior you shall more command with words
> Than with your weapons.

It is inappropriate for a soldier to carry a rusty sword but for a revered old man to put his faith in swords above wisdom—that is piteous: more deeply still Othello is hurt for himself:

> Were it my cue to fight, I should have known it
> Without a prompter.

To miss the acute pain of Othello's embarrassment as early as the bright sword line even is to lose the time-sense of the play and the poignancy of later events when deeds so out of proportion, so entirely inappropriate were performed by the same intelligence. Right through this scene with his father-in-law Othello is found placating a fond and foolish old man, trying to still his fears. All the more sinister does it appear when later we find him implanting fear in others:

> Othello: . . . This hand is moist, my lady.
> Desdemona: It yet hath felt no age nor known no sorrow.

The reader knows what Desdemona does not that she has said what is no longer true. We should ask what dramatic irony really is in terms of the inner relationships of a play—relationships which inform with instant grace and peril every line of it. T. S. Eliot, writing about the line 'Keep up your bright swords,' said it expressed irony, dignity and fearlessness and he added: 'and incidentally it reminds us of the time of night that the scene takes place'.[1] This is linear criticism. He could not have written like this had he asked not only 'What is the time of day?' but also 'What is the time of the play?'

[1] *Poetry and Drama*, p. 29.

He would then have seen the characters not as figures in a morality, but as particular people caught up in particular situations. As Wilson Knight reminds us, *Othello* is a domestic tragedy. We have to make ourselves known then to literature through the recognition of the gradual continuous change that takes place as sentence moves into sentence—in the way our lives move from minutes into hours.

### 14. *Articulacy and Relationship*
If however we are to make the acquaintance of literature in this way, accessibility to our own language resources is essential. We must be articulate for the sake of our authors. And this is a subject in itself. I would like to form a triumvirate: literacy, oracy, articulacy. Articulacy, taken of course in its widest meaning, is a competency we know very little about and this is probably because we may only be able to gain it through suffering inarticulacy, as continuity is often most securely reached through some experience of discontinuity—on the principle of he who shall save his soul must lose it. This is expressed beautifully and cogently in the saying of a Zen master:

Before I was enlightened the rivers were rivers and the mountains were mountains. When I began to be enlightened the rivers were not rivers any more and the mountains were not mountains. Now since I am enlightened the rivers are rivers again and the mountains are mountains.[1]

Perhaps it is because the English lesson plays such a large part in the reclamation and articulation of experience that so many people feel a debt of gratitude to English teachers and the good literature lesson all their lives. But it would not do for these gains to be turned only into the self-absorptive pursuit of personal enlightenment. I have tried to show that it is continuity sought through relationship that truly socializes learning—and through relationships of various orders—through basic trust in

[1] Suzuki, D., *Zen Buddhism and Psycho-analysis*, p. 118.

growth and development—through re-instatement of the self within literature, through reciprocity and fusion—through chronological, simultaneous and integrative modes of cultural awareness, through contact with individual resources along with an absorption of the environment—through the gift to literature of one's own articulacy.

Yet there remains the great paradox that in literature and art events are timed within a timeless world—and consequently the peculiar concern of the literature lesson in particular is to give the child a firm foothold in the fleeting moment.

### 15. *Conclusion*

I was taught at school that one should conclude an essay by looking back to the introduction. I spoke there, you may remember, about the need on the part of young people for help with the problem of continuity within change. Yet I have said less in the paper as a whole about this problem from the child's point of view than from the teacher's angle. This seems to me a proper emphasis in line with the conviction that the child and the adolescent fare best when they have reasonably stable and informed adults to rebel against, when rebel they must. All the same I have referred off and on to the child's understanding of himself and to the rich source of material in children's writings for the student of child development. I will give the adolescent the last word and conclude with a picture from a sixteen-year-old boy of what it feels like to be passing from boyhood into manhood. It is an eloquent comment from the personal point of view upon continuity within change. As with most adolescents he is anxious not to be taken too seriously even when he is claiming all our attention. The title of this poem is:

### THIS I SIP LIGHTLY

We grazed on a little Milton,
Burnt with Donne, and learnt
To spout Eliot, Much of the time
We lived upon a quiet sensitivity,
Spying upon habits, and love,

Trying hard to correlate with poetry.
Browbeaten in arguments, we saw
The masters were there a little lazy,
Here (and mostly here)
Too passionate.

We remembered the
Freedom children have
Of movement; and how, after
Then a word, now an impulse, we were
Changed with the terrible beauty
Of potency, feared to move with so much joy,
For we felt it in our nature's
Tentacles. We thus lived
In restriction
The selective finger of the typist being
No more judicious than we.

Soon we were confirmed
By a board of education, although often
We wondered if we could be such men
As the men in the bank or the teaching staff.
We thus hung with our lacquered habits and motion,
In wonder of the seed.
Considered as a blind symbol, this becomes
'Too intense', as we have called it,
But OUR wonder cannot be called these,
Being careless in its engagement
With the problems. Rarely
Sunk into the ecstasies of desperation, but
Risen to gaze on the sun
With free feeling,
Novice eyes, though not with the intense passion
Of novices.

Soon we shall make serious love to a
Principal university.

Philip Drummond
(Reproduced by kind permission of the
*Daily Mirror* Children's Literary Competition.)

## CONCLUSION

# Further Reflections on Relationship and Growing-up

a. *New understandings*

We have throughout this book been thinking of the teacher-child relationship as a many-sided experience. The teacher, it is thought, should not attempt assessment and judgement until he has first looked at his pupil in the total situation in which they both find themselves. We should be prepared to give a child a fresh start when an appropriate opportunity occurs, whilst our own attitudes to him should be constantly under revision. I heard recently of a teacher who lost one of these opportunities; indeed his type of response is all too common. A young boy had written a first composition after entering the Grammar School. It was entitled 'My Autobiography', and miraculously it seemed as the lines flowed on, he had overcome the lack of fluency which marked his compositions in the Primary School. The boy was filled with a new sense of purpose. He showed me the virgin pages of all his exercise books upon which he was to set his mark. Clean pages, a new school. What an opportunity for a teacher new to the child. In fact the boy got four out of ten with a remark on the poor spelling. His father as a teacher himself understood the need for good standards but he deplored this negative approach at this juncture. He thought of protesting but the boy remarked: 'Leave it alone, he is a teacher, he can't help it.' The reply suggests that although disappointed he was also a little relieved. He had proved something to himself and to his father and perhaps a degree of stringency in the teacher helped him to protect his daring. Many of us thrive best on a mixture of praise and blame, but this is most useful when it comes from the same person and from someone who sees us as a whole. The teacher in question was obviously not aware of the total meaning of this first encounter with the boy. He had failed personally and professionally for it is regrettable when teachers fail to benefit from the social and psychological insights which are now within their reach. We spoke in earlier chapters of the new compassion required of us all today when we are asked to understand behaviour that we do not necessarily condone and to guide young people through the strength of our own self-knowledge. In many respects this new way of thinking is affecting the whole cultural scene through literature and art as well as through psychology and social change in general. Writers and artists are freeing themselves from those edicts which do not adequately take into account the complexity of human nature. Three centuries ago Milton recognized that the question of the liberty of authors was bound up with the problem of our internal struggles. He advised his readers in 'Areopagitica' to recognize in themselves the operation of opposing forces and to face up to the conflicts involved. The statements in question have been embalmed in 'the purple passages' of anthologies whereas they should be taken as a summons to action if we are to avoid a concept of goodness which in Milton's powerful phrase is but 'an excremental whiteness'. 'Good and evil', he tells us, 'grow up together almost inseparably; and the knowledge of good is so involved and interwoven with the knowledge of evil, and in so many cunning resemblances hardly to be discerned that those confused seeds which were imposed upon Psyche as an incessant labour to cull out and sort asunder, were not more inter-mixed.' And further on there comes the call to battle: 'I cannot praise a fugitive and cloistered virtue, unexercised and unbreathed, that never sallies out and meets her adversary but slinks out of the race where that immortal garland is to be run for, not without dust and heat.' It is surely because today we know so much more about the proximity of good and evil, love and hate in man's nature that the teacher's task is changing from one of correction and discipline in the narrow sense to one of guidance in the widest sense.

Perhaps we have cause for optimism for the nearer we get to the recognition of the inter-actions of opposite feelings, the nearer we are to the attainment of harmony—that is if we can learn to sustain conflict and reach beyond compromise to a fine balance of intellect and emotion. Teachers hold a special responsibility in this respect because day in and day out they dispense praise and blame: one of the means by which adjustment is obtained. What is so puzzling and so shocking in our everyday lives is the swiftness with which we turn on these responses. 'A moment is room wide enough.' wrote George Eliot, 'for the loyal and the mean desire, for the outlash of a murderous thought and the sharp backward note of repentance.' Can we learn to intercept that moment so that a truer picture of a situation can emerge? Can we learn to turn an act of admonishment whether of self or of others into a genuine insight into the human state? In practice for the teacher this means finding a way between sentimental involvement and authoritarian detachment. This is not easy because it involves an examination of his own sado-masochistic attitudes. It involves reaching for a true reciprocal relationship, which however is difficult to attain because inevitably one is brought up close to the precarious dependent position of infancy. Yet it is extremely important to acknowledge dependence if true independence is finally to be achieved.

## b. *The Learning Couple*

It is claimed by many child psychologists that the early feeding situation in particular has a profound influence on the child's later development and that the particular experiences of 'the nursing couple' as the early union between mother and child has been called, weave a pattern of relationship which holds in many respects throughout life. Assimilation of food depends, they tell us, upon the whole activity of mothering and not merely upon the management of feeding and defecation at certain hours. And is it not a concern for teaching as a whole that makes for assimilation in learning and not what is somewhat autocratically called 'classroom management'? Further than this a more mysterious link arises between mother and child, teacher and pupil when questions of identity are involved. The way the mother thinks about herself will affect the way the baby begins to think of himself. This mutually identifying aspect of later learning was dwelt upon to some extent in the last chapter. We saw for example in the instance of 'the good reading lesson' that it is through a sense of the teacher's closeness to his own resources that the child comes to learn about his own.

It is clear all the same that 'the nursing couple' is not likely to be well adjusted all the time; and teachers too are bound at times to foresake teaching as an intuitional or deeply pondered procedure, and have recourse to technique alone which of course can never have more than a limited value. Programmed learning for example is a useful way of preparing material to be readily assimilated, but we still have to look for social and personal incentives. Children seem to take in knowledge far more deeply when they are aware of its being enjoyed and grasped by someone else: whilst teaching children is one of the best ways of gaining knowledge for oneself. There is nothing new here, yet it is extremely difficult to let these things happen in practice. It involves allowing children to observe us as closely as we observe them. This can be very disconcerting for children have a relentless regard for truth. However, a healthy child gains much from the incorporation of the grown-ups' own efforts at assimilation. A student told me during a school practice that he had noticed how whenever he was talking with a class and a new idea came into his mind that he himself had not yet assimilated it was precisely this point that they queried first. He noticed too that when he accepted their challenge and moulded the new material into the subsequent discussion the class responded adventurously. They were then prepared to risk their own ideas.

Although the question of the relation between reciprocity and assimilation has not been given much attention as yet in educational theory and practice it has for some time been a major concern of psycho-analysis—whilst recently it has been brought into prominence by a number of distinguished art critics—notably by Professor E. Gombrich, and Adrian Stokes—both quoted in the last chapter. Gombrich has in several places described the emergence of an attitude towards art whereby we repeat the artist's imaginative performance in our own minds—'we are drawn into the charmed circle and share in the secret.'[1] The audience, he insists, is part of the work of art. In the deeply considered essay already referred to, *The Invitation in Art*, Stokes discloses the very complex way in which we relate to works of art especially when we are strongly attracted to them.[2] He speaks of how when enveloped by a work of art we meet with the invitation 'to enjoy subsequently as a nourishment our own corresponding processes.'[3] That is to say it is through 'the compelling invitation to identify', as he puts it, that we ultimately know ourselves as separate beings. He refers to Marion Milner's observation that a state of oneness is a necessary step in the apprehension of two-ness. From the point of view of the curriculum it is mainly in the study of the humanities where appreciation plays such a large part that these subtle relationships make themselves felt yet in the sciences too the stage of being enveloped in a problem is necessary to subsequent objective evaluation, whilst the discovery of an invitation to problem solving is one of the strongest incentives to learning of any kind.

For more precise information on the means whereby we enter these magic circles of art and learning we need to return to our model of babyhood—this time it is in the toddler-parent relationship that we are most likely to gain the clearest picture—where we can see how ideas of separation are encouraged in the child by the ability to walk and in some measure to talk. But he needs assurance not only through word of mouth or by a gesture on the part of the parents, he needs to gain it through a trust in

---

[1] *Meditations on a Hobby Horse*, 1963, p. 37.

[2] Throughout the essay Stokes acknowledges how much his ideas have been influenced by the work of Melanie Klein.

[3] p. 19.

the mother he is taking into himself as he separates from her and one way in which he does this is to perform with his objects those essential mothering acts which were performed with him. In short he ritualizes the act of mothering and thus ensures an 'entrée' into a rich and varied world.

It is all too easy to miss the extraordinary delicacy of these little acts which so soon pass into the broad activity of dramatic play. One day I came upon a little girl of one year six months enacting such a little drama by her mother's bedside. The mother was mildly indisposed, and it was unusual for Caroline to find her in bed in the day time. She took a newspaper from the bed, put it on the floor and placed her teddy bear upon it—then she mimed with great precision the movements her mother made when changing her nappies. My attention was drawn to the formal movements, ritualistically carried out. It was, the mother told me soon after this, on the same day in fact, that she sat on her pot for the first time. There is of course a great deal that could be discussed here but those familiar with the work of Dr. D. W. Winnicott will recognize this incident as an example of the kind of reciprocal communication he has dealt with in his now famous article on 'Transitional Objects and Transitional Phenomena. (1951)'[1] Here he traces a baby's play activity from the fist in the mouth, through the first 'not me' possessions such as a piece of sheet or blanket through to the attachment to a teddy, doll or hard toy—all of which he regards as signs of progress in the baby's ability to separate from its mother and give up his early oral and anal attachments to her. So the child's first play with these transitional objects becomes a symbol of an important stage in relationship. In a later article Winnicott thinks of transitional objects in terms of culture.[2] He notes the significance of the juncture between being one with the mother and separating from her—the significance as he puts it of the point of their initiation into separateness. In fact he sees us as contributing

[1] *Collected Papers*. Tavistock Publications Ltd, 1958, pp. 229 ff.
[2] 'The Location of Cultural experience', Chapter VII, in *Playing and Reality*, pp. 95–103, 1971, Tavistock.

to a cultural heritage at the moment of discovering ourselves. However, further significance is given to this idea when the full value of the formal and ritualistic aspects of this transition are appreciated. The little girl only needed the newspaper—the symbol for protection of the object—and miming did the rest. By this means she was becoming the mother of *her* baby and thus releasing her own mother from her tasks. Obviously there would be many returns to the dependent position—but a stage had been reached—and in Winnicott's terms the location of cultural experience, entailing innovation and tradition had been set down. As well what Stokes calls 'an incantatory process'—was being employed as a means of communicating these quite complex matters to the family. It was about this time that Caroline began to use words with discernable purpose. In a way she was engaging in a pact between the past and the future through an act of the present.

The formal aspects of communication found in song and dance, in mime and alliteration, rhyme and rhythm, and so on are wonderful spurs to aesthetic achievement but they can of course become debased and turn into obsessions. When a child day in and day out acts out the same dramas without variation we have cause for alarm; (and of course when a lecturer repeatedly gives the same lecture). On the other hand it is possible that we have neglected the value of certain formal aspects of learning in an attempt to gain freedom from obsessive pursuits, that we have failed to see the connection between formal procedures and the heightened perception, the attention to detail which they bring about—'a relationship through whose power each content in the work of art can be deeply communicated.'[1] Thus it is important in our treatment of texts for us to identify with a 'sense of process in action' if we are to reach the work in all its detail and manifold reference. Attention to content alone is like attempting to study a tree by bumping into it.

We have in the argument of the last few pages tried to bring notions of continuity and reciprocity in learning together by

[1] *The Invitation in Art*, p. 18.

taking as our model first the nursing couple and then the toddler in process of separation from the mother. It is however at adolescence when social considerations come to the fore that the picture most markedly changes—for this is a time when our creative capabilities are put to the test. Yet the beginning of it all lies in the story of Caroline who by an act of independence ran the risk in her feelings of losing her cherished union with her mother. Undoubtedly her courage came from the trust she had assimilated at the breast—during the early most dependent stage of her life. Her action spoke the words: This you did for me, this I can now do for you.

## c. *The Self in Transformation*

The most striking factor about the learning adolescent is that he not only knows or does not know, but he knows that he knows or does not know. Knowledge and ignorance are 'felt in the blood and felt along the heart'. If learning is progressing well, self-discovery inevitably takes place and a sense arises of what the French psychologist Herbert Fingarette has called; 'the self in transformation.'[1] The urge to reconstitute the self through the resolution of conflict is very strong in the adolescent, and by this time many forms of expression are open to him, if he can take advantage of them. We talk much about the inhibitions and irresponsibilities of members of this age-group but as yet we seem to know little about the extent of their awareness of their own psychic lives. The amazing development in recent years of children's own writing and of their work in the arts is providing us, as we saw in the last chapter, with a great deal of material for study—if we can learn to make use of it.

For example the following poem written by a boy of fifteen furnishes an eloquent statement on the relation between conflict and the acceptance of truth. He is describing a relationship between a boy and a bird who visited his garden. In these verses the writer is fully aware of the issues at stake when we

[1] Herbert Fingarette, *The Self in Transformation*, Basic Books, 1963.

have to grapple with the sadness and anger which the loss of our
loved objects brings about.

## HIS BIRD

Each day at three, he returned to
The sunken garden, where he found
His little bird, three days before,
His lovely multi-coloured bird,
That piped and spoke so sweet to him.
Each day he saw his friend who too
Befriended him. 'Hello Hello',
He used to cry with song so gay.
His birdy spoke so many things,
His beauty answered questionings
He dared not put to anyone.
The little boy knew everything,
Now that his bird had told him all,
His bird sang words that rang so true,
And yet his bird was one that flew,
With tripping trill, shrill melody.
Notes of truth in mellow tone,
Truth in notes of melody,
He heard, yet could not have
His bird, he grasped his words,
Yet could not grasp his form:
He did not ask to pet
His bird, but yet he knew
Him well—his eyes adored
His form, not hands that stroked
The down, his mind absorb'd
The words, not ears the sound.

'You know, you know,' his birdy cried,
'Goodbye, goodbye, I am going.'
No more did tunes replenish trees
And plants, that hungry stood beside
His garden, where he sat and cried.
The leaf he frayed,

The sticks he laid
In order, stayed
There still. The ground
He knew, the round
Bush, some stone found
Remained.

But his little bird had flown,
His lovely little coloured bird,
His sweetly singing ring-necked bird,
The birdlet that he called his own.

He cried and wept his bird.

'He flew to the sun, you took him,
You were the thief, you stole my bird.
My yellow bird flew to the sun,
The yellow sun received my bird.
The sun took him away from me.'

He sighed and slept awhile.

He knew, yet had not clutched him close,
He felt with him, but had not felt.
He saw him not, but kept with him
The spirit of his bird, now gone.
The bird was his, and yet he was
The sun's: he was the sun's as well,
The sun was his to know, for now
He had heard, and he could know all.

Up from the well of his sorrow
He drew his joy, for great the depth
Of sorrow, hollowed in himself,
Contained great depths of joy unmasked.
This little boy
Through grief knew joy,
Through songs of bird,

He knew he heard
A wisdom of the world.
His bird had gone,
Who was the one,
Who made him sad,
But now he had
A realm of truth unfurled.
'My bird, my sun, I know.'
He laughed and loved the world.

Duncan A. Forbes[1]

The writer has traced a developing experience through five phases. In the first he sets the time and the scene in which a relationship grows up between the boy and the bird. Then the bird announces his departure. The loss is shared with the plants and the trees and yet the apartness of objects, their self sufficiency, serve as reminders of his own desolation. The boy croons to himself; he sorrows and mourns for his multi-coloured bird, until at last his anger breaks forth. His loved one has been unfaithful to him. He has gone over to the Sun. Slowly the realization that he can share this partnership quietens him. He takes 'the spirit of his bird now gone' into himself, and draws joy out of sorrow with the explicit knowledge that he is learning about the truth. Truth he realizes comes in slow stages but it is unlikely to come at all without a willingness to bring opposite feelings together; in this case the love and the hate felt for the bird who has both befriended him and deserted him. This discovery is in line with a statement of Dr Bion's about the precondition for truth acceptance—'to have the view of an object which is hated enjoined with the view of the same object when it is loved.' Such conjunctions Bion tells us feed us with the truth, and he points out that in these terms we can suffer from truth starvation.[2] According to Hannah Segal it is only

[1] From *Children as Writers*, Book V. pp. 35–37. Reproduced by kind permission of the 'Daily Mirror' Children's Literary Competition.

[2] 'A Theory of Thinking', by W. R. Bion. 1962. *I.J.P.A.*—July–Oct. pp. 306 ff.

when the loss of a beloved object has been acknowledged and the mourning experienced that re-creation can take place. She quotes Proust: 'On ne peut recréer ce qu'on aime qu'en le renonçant'. ('It is only by renouncing that one can recreate what one loves'.)[1]

But as well as describing the re-creation of the lost object, the author of 'His Bird' is speaking of what we used to call 'sublimation'—the transmutation of mainly sensuous experience into words and concepts.

> . . . not hands that stroked
> The down, his mind absorb'd
> The words, not ears the sound.

And we thought of this taking place rather miraculously and suddenly at adolescence. Now we know that change is gradual and continuous, though it has its spurts as at puberty; besides we think more in terms of 'socialization' which the boy poet experiences as coming from a willingness to share our love with others.

> The bird was his and yet he was
> The sun's: he was the sun's as well.

In terms of family life the child's readiness to find a place in his feelings for both his parents and *their* relationship is followed by closer contacts with brothers and sisters, and later with school-mates. 'He laughed and loved the world.'

All the same this harmony, so beautifully celebrated in the poem, does not always take place, with the result that many problems appropriate to one stage of development get carried on to the next. To some extent we live anacronistically. It is not to be wondered at that schools reflect so many of our immaturities and give us so much to unlearn. Both children and teachers for instance may unwittingly transfer to their class-mates and colleagues respectively those aspects of sibling rivalry that were not worked through in the nursery.

[1] 'A psycho-analytic approach to aesthetics', *I.J.P.A.* Vol. XXXIII, 1952, p. 199.

### d. *A Community of Fate*

In order to gain a true picture of school life we need to take positive and negative features together. A striking feature of most schools is the amount of creative endeavour that goes on in spite of much frustration. To some extent we all harbour a grudge against our school days even though we are also aware of how much we enjoyed them. For are not schools the places we were sent to, with very little say on our part, and away from the constant comforts and securities of home? Children in boarding schools may score here for their grudge is more easily rationalized. People make a big mistake when they attempt to idealize a child's reaction to school life dwelling solely on the happiness and satisfactions which are undoubtedly there but overlooking the deep resentment which is part of the adult's task to help him to overcome. Homes and schools are the only places where 'grudgery' can be tolerated in love and affection. Children may think they have a right to rail against parents and teachers (often playing them off against each other) because they know they would defend them against outside criticism. It happens sometimes however that children from 'good homes' and 'good' schools have to postpone their resentments until the next separation crisis, that is until they enter the outside world. Thus they avoid an attack on the good parents and teachers and turn it in however disguised a form upon society. Most children want to preserve their right to belong, but some find it difficult to rid themselves of the belief that all alliances are formed against them. Adolescents have a tendency to join a gang thus gaining within a chosen group protection against those threatening alliances over which they have no control.

Teachers too may within their alliances be seeking refuge against a society from which they feel alienated. Many grudges then take place in one part of the feelings of children and teachers whilst in another part they value highly the advantages of learning and teaching. Once the ambivalent attitude towards schools is brought into the light then there is more hope for the future; for schools can provide a much needed breathing space within which groups of people with common interests can learn from each other. We have underestimated the benefits which companionship amongst children and colleagueship amongst teachers can bestow. Many children have the most astonishing understanding of each other and of themselves as developing human beings which makes them very sensitive to both deprivation and giftedness in others. This insight could be the teacher's greatest ally but we are only just releasing children from those serried rows of desks where they have been prevented from communicating with each other. Similarly teachers are only just beginning to explore the possibilities of groupings within their own ranks.

The phrase in the sub-title above, 'community of fate', was in fact employed by the sociologist Erving Goffman to help him to differentiate between team workers and colleagues. A team, he explains, is brought together for the accomplishment of a common purpose. Colleagues do not share the same work but the same 'community of fate'.[1] With having to put on the same kind of performance they come to know each other's difficulties and points of view. So he sees a team worker as much more closely bound to his co-workers than a colleague is. Here one can see something of the limitation of the sociological approach when taken on its own. D. W. Harding in a review of Goffman's book, *The Presentation of Self in Everyday Life* remarks upon the absence of the self-concept: 'He rejects with amusement,' Harding writes, 'the notion that there is any "individual" self not constructed out of social roles'. Goffman would perhaps be even more likely to reject the notion of a reciprocal learning relationship acting as a strengthener to this individual self. Colleagues may in fact be drawn together on the basis of a shared interest in this very relationship, one which makes for 'a teamship of the spirit' rather than for 'a team spirit'. Teachers do most devoutly seek after kindred spirits. A teacher's life is pretty irksome and confining, and being with children day in and day out is very exhausting. Maybe I have brought the ideas in these various

[1] *The Presentation of Self in Everyday Life,* p. 140.

articles together under one cover to try and explain why teachers go on teaching since their status in society is not very high. They have told me hundreds of times, what I have experienced for myself over and over again, that if there is a chance once a week, once every so often, to share with children and colleagues some of those moments of vision which learning affords—a chance to take on the spirit of meaning and sense the presence of 'something far more deeply interfused'—

> A motion and a spirit, that impels
> All thinking things, all objects of all thought,
> And rolls through all things.'

that if there is the occasional opportunity to do this, then there is no profession in the world with which they would exchange their own. Teachers who never have this experience should perhaps pack up and go for their own sakes as well as for the sake of the children; but for those who do, society should be geared to help them to make full use of it and to turn a community of fate into a community of choice.

This is perhaps a good point to look with the learner's eye and to ask oneself when it was in one's own schooling or university career that one became aware of these 'moving spirits' about which Wordsworth reports so accurately—when in fact one became aware of being educated. I have in mind my own experience when in the lecture room, in the small seminar group I felt a communion between my mind and that of my professor—which seemed to be shared with my fellow students—a communion which took one into the heart of the text under discussion in a way that was as enlarging and social as it was private and individual; as deeply compassionate as it was justly critical. These qualities were transferred mainly through the voice, conveying a fine overall integrity rather than any adapted critical stand-point—though scholarly standards and attention to detail were not wanting.

I have spoken in various contexts within these pages of the

value of allowing for a conjuncture of near and far, closeness and apartness, particular and universal. This conjuncture is known to people in love and I believe to all people at times when through the pressure of mutual need, the fact of a man's eventual isolation is borne in upon them. Life is a process of distancing as we grow closer. It is easier to accept the teacher's apartness than the parent's; whilst next in turn it may be easier for some children to accept more abstract forms of learning than those where a teacher is personally involved. Children who cannot bring near and far together may try to repudiate learning altogether; but for those who can there are endless voyages of discovery. For the sensitive child however there will always be some pain when he is brought up before 'the other life' of the teacher—though not as deep as the pain he felt when he realized that his parents had a life of their own apart from himself: yet hurt is there all the same and accessible for instance to this seven year old Japanese child.

> The day snow blew down from the black valley
> my teacher was standing by the stove.
> I wanted to call, 'Teacher'
> but I couldn't because she seemed to be angry.
> My teacher was staring outside
> and in her eyes you could see the white storm.
>
> Kuramitsu Miyuki[1]

This is poetry, but it also marks the beginning of a critical attitude to life. In the end most children become reconciled to the loss of their illusions for knowledge in itself generates hope.

> Whate'er exists hath properties that spread
> Beyond itself, communicating good,
> A simple blessing, or with evil mixed;
> Spirit that knows no insulated spot,
> No chasm, no solitude; from link to link

[1] From *There are Two Lives*. Poems by children of Japan edited by Richard Lewis, translated by Haruna Kimura. Simon & Schuster, New York.

It circulates, the soul of all the worlds.
This is the freedom of the universe;
Unfolded still the more, more visible
The more we know; and yet is reverenced least,
And least respected in the human mind,
Its most apparent home. The food of hope
Is meditated action; robbed of this
Her sole support, she languishes and dies.
We perish also; for we live by hope
And by desire; we see by the glad light
And breathe the sweet air of futurity;
And so we live, or else we have no life.[1]

[1] *The Poetical Works of William Wordsworth,* 'The Excursion,' Book Nine, lines 10–26. Oxford edition (1920).

# Select References

Allen, W., *Tradition and Dream*, 1964, Phoenix House.

Bion, W. R., *A Theory of Thinking*, 1962, *I.J.P.A.*

Charon, J. E., *Man in Search of Himself*, 1967, translated from the French by J. E. Anderson, George Allen & Unwin Ltd.

Cox, C. B. and Dyson, A. E., 1. 'Fight for Education', 1968: *The Critical Quarterly*, 2. 'Crisis in Education', 1970, *The Critical Quarterly*.

Eliot, T. S., *Poetry and Drama*, 1951, Faber & Faber.

Eisenstein, S., *The Film Sense*, 1948, 2nd ed., Faber & Faber.

Fingarette, H., *The Self in Transformation*, 1963, Basic Books U.S.A.

Freud, S., *The Interpretation of Dreams*, 1932, 3rd English ed.

Goffman, E., *The Presentation of Self in Everyday Life*, 1969, Allen Lane, The Penguin Press.

Gombrich, E., *Meditations on a Hobby Horse*, 1963, Phaidon Press.

Hourd, M. L. and Cooper, G., *Coming Into Their Own*, 1959, paperback 1971, Heinemann Educational Books.

Milner, M., *On Not Being Able to Paint*, 2nd edition, 1957, paperback 1971, Heinemann Educational Books.

Morris, B., 'Inspection as Leadership through Guidance'—*The New Era in Home and School*. Nov. 1955.

Richardson, E., *Group Study for Teachers*, 1967, Routledge & Kegan Paul.

Segal, H., '*A Psycho-analytic Approach to Aesthetics*,' 1952, *I.J.P.A.*, Vol. XXXIII.

Steiner, G., 'A Conversation with Claude Lévi-Strauss', April 1966, *Encounter*.

Stokes, A., *The Invitation in Art*, 1965, Tavistock Publications.

Suzuki, C., *Zen Buddhism and Psycho-analysis*, 1960, George Allen & Unwin.

Winnicott, D. W., *Collected Papers*, 1958, Tavistock Publications. 'The Location of Cultural Experience', Chapter VII in 'Playing and Reality', pp. 95–103, 1971, Tavistock. *The Child the Family and the Outside World*, 1964, Penguin Books.

# Index of Names

# Index of Subjects